LOST SKI AREAS

of

Tahoe and Donner

LOST SKI AREAS

of

Tahoe and Donner

INGRID P. WICKEN

THE History PRESS

Published by The History Press
Charleston, SC
www.historypress.com

Cover images courtesy of Donner Summit Historical Society, Norm Sayler Collection; Karen Stangland; Lake Tahoe Historical Society; and the author's collection.

First published 2020

Manufactured in the United States

ISBN 9781467140584

Library of Congress Control Number: 2020941800

Notice: The information in this book is true and complete to the best of our knowledge. It is offered without guarantee on the part of the author or The History Press. The author and The History Press disclaim all liability in connection with the use of this book.

For Karen M. Buettner and Lynne D. Barrett.
Here's to ski adventures of years gone by and forty-five years of friendship.

CONTENTS

ACKNOWLEDGEMENTS

This book is the result of a genuinely combined effort of many people. A number of individuals made vital contributions to this project, and without the information and images they provided, this book would not have been possible. My greatest thanks and appreciation to Molly Beucus for help with securing documents and images from the Donner Summit Historical Society; Bill Clark, Auburn Ski Club and the Western Skisport Museum, for providing information and photographs of the Cisco area; Therese Dunn, librarian of the Sierra Club Colby Library, for assisting with Sierra Club ski history and providing leads in the old *Sierra Club Bulletins*; Gigi Heckendorn for her help with the history of Hoyfjellet Lodge; Janet Hildebrand, granddaughter of Joel Hildebrand, and Christopher W. Klein, son of Louise Hildebrand Klein and Ferdinand (Fred) Klein, and nephew of Bill Klein, for sharing the Hildebrand/Klein family skiing history and sending the fantastic photographs of Joel Hildebrand and Bill and Fred Klein; Diana Homsey, daughter of George Homsey, for the spectacular photographs, stories and book about her father and his contributions to skiing at Clair Tappaan Lodge; Diane L. Johnson, Lake Tahoe Historical Society, for her assistance in finding lost ski area photographs and ephemera in the museum collections; Bill Kier, former part-owner of the Strawberry Lodge, for his personal story in the history of the lodge and for the book on Strawberry's history; Laurie Krill, acquisitions editor for The History Press, who provided valuable advice and guidance every step of the way; Nina Eggen McLeod, who, with Dave Wakeman, spent a morning with me on a driving tour of

Highway 50 scouting the locations of lost ski areas; Chaun Morier, Truckee Donner Historical Society, for helping with the history of Hilltop skiing; Bill Oudegeest, for assisting with the history of skiing at Serene Lakes and helping to provide images from Norm Sayler's collection; Jimmy Petterson, whose parents, Bill and Reserl Petterson, were pioneer ski instructors at Strawberry Lodge and Strawberry Ski Hut—Jimmy provided many photographs and anecdotes of his parents' days at Strawberry; Doug Pfeiffer, for reviewing and editing the manuscript. His comments and corrections always result in vast improvements to the story and the way that it is told. Melinda Pillsbury-Foster, for the photograph of her grandfather Arthur C. Pillsbury; Russ Potts, for sharing his family's history of the Burroughs Resort; Eric and Wayne Poulsen, for sharing their dad's story, not just at Squaw Valley but also Papoose Ski Area; Michael Rettie, for the use of his extraordinary cache of Lewis Clark photographs of early Donner Summit skiing; Norm Sayler, founder of the Donner Summit Historical Society—Norm has encyclopedic knowledge of the Donner Summit area and was my go-to source for information and fact checking on Highway 40 ski areas; Karen Stangland, daughter of Gordon and Harriet Stangland, who founded the Nebelhorn with Vic West—Karen generously shared the Stangland family scrapbook and other Nebelhorn memorabilia, adding greatly to the written and visual history of the area; Carol Van Etten, Lake Tahoe historian and author; Bill Briner, photographer, for his only-known photograph of the Lake Tahoe Ski Club area at Tahoe City; Dave Wakeman, who has skied many of Tahoe's lost ski areas, for his extensive knowledge and memories of all of the old Highway 50 areas; and Kay Wells, former wife of George Homsey, for sharing her personal anecdotes and history of skiing at the Sierra Club Signal Hill ski tow. And the warmest of thanks to my dear friend Lynne D. Barrett, who generously provided a place to stay and good company on all of my research trips.

INTRODUCTION

Around Lake Tahoe, along U.S. Highway 50 and U.S. Highway 40 (now Interstate 80), a number of California's pioneer ski areas were founded and developed from the 1930s through the 1950s. Those two major highways began as pack trails and wagon roads when immigrants and fortune seekers began making their way west to California. With the mining came lumbering, general stores, transportation and eventually recreation and tourism. Camps and towns were developed to supply and support the mines and miners. The pioneers who settled and stayed year-round north of Tahoe in Johnsville and LaPorte are famous for the longboard races they staged in the nineteenth century.

But most nineteenth-century residents of the Sierra were using their skis for practical purposes rather than for sport. Skis were vital to winter life in California mountains. The exploits of Snowshoe Thompson carrying the mail from Placerville to Genoa in the 1860s has become legend. John R. Gillis, a railroad engineer, wrote of skis' importance to the work on the Central Pacific Railroad:

> *We started with Canadian snowshoes, but soon abandoned them for the Norwegian, each a strip of light wood ten to twelve feet long, four inches wide, and an inch and a quarter thick in the center; they taper in thickness toward the end, are turned up in front, and grooved on the bottom. There is a broad strap in the middle to put the foot under, and a balancing-pole to steady, push, and brake with. The latter will be seen all-important, as a speed of twenty-five to thirty miles an hour is often attained on a steep hill-side.*[1]

At the turn of the twentieth century, winter tourism at Lake Tahoe was virtually nonexistent. Resorts were summer-only operations because of heavy snowfall blanketing the primitive roads into the area. The forest highway program in the 1930s led to improved paved highways such as Highway 50 to the south shore and state routes 89 and 28 to the western, northern and eastern shores of Lake Tahoe.

Transportation either by train or by automobile was the key to the development of winter sports areas in and around Lake Tahoe. Initially rail travel and eventually improved roads led to the opening of the Sierra to winter tourists. This was especially true in Northern California with Highway 40. Prior to 1932, when heavy snow blanketed roads, skiers were thwarted from reaching the best slopes for skiing. Once snow removal brought about winter access, ski tows sprang up anywhere there was sufficient snow and open slopes.

But Californians were also tasked with overcoming the decades-long publicity by the California State Chamber of Commerce touting sunny California as a Mediterranean escape from cold and snow. By the end of the 1920s, the chamber had a new attitude toward winter sports. In 1929, it began an aggressive campaign to formally organize, promote and support skiing in California. *Ski Illustrated* magazine reported,

> *Recognizing the value of winter sports as a trade and travel stimulation, the State Chamber of Commerce of California devoted a major part of their program to the planning and coordinating of snow activities throughout the state.…Enthusiastic support was given the plan to tell the Winter Sports Story of California as well as its summer vacation and sunshine attractions and thus double the vacation appeal.*[2]

By 1934, so many ski areas lined Highway 40 from Emigrant Gap to Soda Springs the area was dubbed "Winter Sports Supreme." Those areas drew skiers from near and far, and Cisco Grove grew to be the largest and most popular among skiers. It was home to the Auburn Ski Club, which developed ski jumping hills, cleared downhill runs and built a warming hut and other facilities catering to skiers. According to ski historian Bill Berry, Cisco was "Northern California's first developed ski area."[3]

Many attributed the booming popularity of Tahoe and Donner winter sports to the snow trains, but a 1937 *Oakland Tribune* article offered this take on the rise of skiing:

> *Some claimed it was the weekend snow trains to Truckee and Yosemite. Others saw the rise of ski-mindedness as a direct and logical result of intensive advertising by Yosemite-Camp Curry and by the ski jumping exhibitions put on at the University of California campus by the Auburn Ski Club and the State Chamber of Commerce, but this could hardly have accounted for all the tremendous travel to Cisco, to Badger Pass, to Truckee, to Soda Springs and many other fine ski fields in the Sierras. The true cause was simple and an obvious one: beginning in November the news-stands blossomed forth with magazine covers after cover with ski pictorials and information on Winter resorts and apparel within their covers. The* Tribune *published its first Winter Sports edition in the middle of January, as well as a daily Winter sports column.*[4]

Skiers who frequented the areas closer to Lake Tahoe were drawn to the magnificence of the scenery. Oliver Kehrlein, ski writer for the *San Francisco Examiner*, described the extraordinary beauty that Lake Tahoe afforded skiers:

> *By those who know it in its winter garb, Lake Tahoe is considered the gem of America's winter sports areas. Here, in addition to the snow-covered peaks and great green forests, the skier has the largest mountain lake on our continent, as a panoramic background to his trackless trail. The ever-changing temperaments of the winter sky are continually reflected in its deep waters extending 30 miles to the great mountain ranges opposite.*[5]

The first boom in California skiing took place in the 1930s but came to a virtual standstill during World War II. But once the war was over and life began to return to normal, skiing resumed with a fervor and experienced an even greater boom. A number of factors played into this growth: automobile travel (no gas rationing, rubber tires again available, better roads, more car ownership), the Forest Service cooperating with private developers on forest lands, winter roads kept open and free of snow and the advent of the ski lift. Ski tows and lifts were a relatively new innovation in the 1930s, but they were no longer a novelty after the war. During the 1946–47 season, there were sixty-seven tows and lifts operating in California, and a third of those were in the Tahoe and Donner area: fifteen in the Tahoe National Forest and seven in the El Dorado National Forest.

The magnitude of the postwar boom in California skiing was summed up in a *New York Times* article:

> *The perpetual to-do about California's sunshine, warmth, and palm trees generally obscures the fact that the Golden State also possesses unquestionably the most extensive array of winter resorts of any state in the union. On many of California's mountain heights, snow reigns the whole year round. During the six months of winter and spring there extends, over the 1,000-mile expanse from the Oregon line to the Mexican border, an almost continuous chain of snowsports centers, comprising more than 100 sites in around thirty different districts.*[6]

By 1949, Highway 40, also known as the Donner Trail, had grown to be the number-one ski locale in the state. There were accommodations for 3,000 skiers and approximately 22,000 feet of cable and rope for T-bars, J-bars, a chairlift and rope tows. Wolfgang Lert commented that "Transcontinental Highway 40, with its string of tows, lifts and lodges from Auburn to the Donner Ski Ranch at the summit of Donner Pass, makes one doubt that anyone could travel through here in winter and not become a skier."[7] From Baxter's to Truckee, there were many points in between that operated tows to attract the winter crowds: Laing's Pioneer Camp, Yuba Gap, Cisco, Rainbow Tavern and Soda Springs, to name a few. During these ski destinations' heyday, as many as 220,000 snow sports enthusiasts visited Highway 40 areas in a single season.

Highway 40 and Highway 50 were the two most important east–west highways in terms of opening up winter sports terrain in the Tahoe area. Local business owners formed organizations to foster and promote skiing and lodging. One such group was the Sierra Loop organization, formed during the 1949–50 season. It was created for those who owned or managed resorts, hotels and lodges with ski slopes, or lifts and tows. Split into four geographic zones, two members from each zone made up the committee. Glen Myers was appointed the general chairman with the executive committee as follows: Highway 40, Gordon Hooley and Charles Van Evera; Reno, Keston Ramsey and Bill Cashill; Lake Tahoe, Bill Bliss and Barbara Pinney; and Highway 50, Gordon Stangland and Ken Cotton. The primary objective of the Sierra Loop group was "to introduce to the public in general, through publicity, advertising and service, the facilities that have been developed to accommodate the skiing public in the Sierra Loop."[8]

Tahoe ski areas proliferated in the 1950s, and in December 1960, ski journalists "Kit" Carson White and Don "Snowshoe" Thompson made a one-day ski excursion of Tahoe and Donner ski areas. On their "Tahoe Ski Marathon," as they called it, they visited four gondolas, twenty-five chairlifts,

Left: Brochure promoting the many ski areas along the Sierra Loop. *Courtesy of the Lake Tahoe Historical Society.*

Below: Map of the Sierra Loop, highlighting what Carson White and Don Thompson dubbed "the world's greatest ski complex." *Courtesy of the Lake Tahoe Historical Society.*

eleven platter pulls, thirty-seven rope tows and two T-bars. At the end of their ski marathon, White summed up the virtues of Tahoe skiing:

> *We graphically showed that Lake Tahoe ski complex is all one area. Vacationist could spend two weeks without skiing the same place twice. The beautiful jewel, Lake Tahoe, has plenty to offer and the fun spots at Reno and Southshore* [sic] *are an unbeatable combination. Easterners should be told this. Even more Californians should be made aware of the world's greatest ski complex, Lake Tahoe.*[9]

And, in December 1973, Morten Lund wrote, "In the territory around the lake bounded by Carson and Donner Passes is the greatest single concentration of lifts in the world. The multiple folds of Sierra skiing around Lake Tahoe contain 22 ski areas, with 146 lifts, including 78 chairlifts—all sitting only 150 miles due east of San Francisco on Interstate 80, four lanes all the way."[10]

This book will explore the origins of skiing along the Sierra Loop: the Lake Tahoe basin, Highway 50 and Highway 40. These two pioneer trans-Sierra roads are heavily used today, and few passersby would realize historic ski tows and lifts stretched for miles along these highways. Prior to examining the origins of Tahoe and Donner lost ski areas, the stories of the intrepid skiers who ventured into the mountains around Lake Tahoe long before there were any ski lifts will be told. Then, the history of the many pioneer ski resorts and tows that helped to usher in the boom in postwar skiing in Northern California is recounted. The origin and development of these areas and some of the factors that led to their demise will be examined. These early ski areas paved the way for today's large resorts that draw millions of snow sports enthusiasts every winter. And these lost ski areas marked the beginning of the Tahoe and Donner area becoming the skiing mecca that it is today.

1

BEFORE THERE WERE TOWS

In the nineteenth century, the few residents who wintered at Lake Tahoe utilized skis for travel, hunting and other activities vital for living in mountains in winter. There are a handful of written accounts documenting these early experiences on skis.

E.B. Scott, in his book *The Saga of Lake Tahoe*, chronicled some of these early skiers and their feats on skis. In January 1874, fifteen residents remained in Tahoe City. During the long winter months, they hunted and trapped white hare, fox and marten. Joseph B. Campbell, a Tahoe City businessman, snowshoed (skied) into Truckee, making the sixteen-mile trip over the snow-covered road in six hours.

In the 1880s, Jim McNutt was the year-round caretaker at Deer Park Inn, located on the west shore of Lake Tahoe. It was reported that McNutt "could take a pair of spring hickory staves, rub their running surfaces smooth, smear them with bear fat, pick a steep tree-covered slope of powder snow and leave both the guff-and-blow braggart and experienced cross-country skier behind in a whirling white barrage."[11] Because of these and other outdoor feats, he was labeled "the hardest man to follow in the Sierra."[12]

Thomas Magee, prominent San Francisco real estate mogul, was undoubtedly the first Californian to make annual winter visits to Lake Tahoe, specifically to engage in backcountry skiing. He started making these annual excursions around 1880, continuing into the mid-1890s. He was also the first to advocate for winter as well as summer visits to Lake

Tahoe, writing, "The Sierra Nevada Mountains are California's greatest winter attraction." He continued,

> *I have for years made it a practice to visit the upper Sierra in winter on snowshoes, and I hold, and in this opinion there will be no dissent from those who live in the mountains, that there is no other season comparable to winter for wildness of beauty of woods, hardy magnificence of scenery, bracing climate and sky and cloud contrasts and splendor. One winter week in the Sierra on snowshoes, spending each whole day in the open air, is worth at least a month there in summer.*[13]

In March 1896, Magee and three companions—Robert Watson, George Honsucker Jr. and Jim McNutt—began a ski tour that would take them from Lake Tahoe via Ward's Creek to Summit Station on Donner Summit. Twenty years prior, Magee and John Muir hiked the opposite direction from Summit Station to Lake Tahoe, inspiring him to someday make the trip on skis.

By the time the group made it to Deer Park Canyon, rain and poor weather forced the group to stay at McNutt's house for thirty-six hours. Once the weather cleared, they set out again. They started at night and reached the summit at one o'clock in the afternoon. They skied around the base of Anderson Peak and worked their way down into the canyon of the American River, finishing their tour at Soda Springs. They reached Soda Springs after nine and a half hours of steep ascents and descents.

Magee reported on the terrain the group faced the next day:

> *Some of the slopes we encountered in descending the mountains were over half a mile in length, and were excessively steep. Even our best men had to sit down on their snowshoes in the descent, while I, less experienced and far more awkward, used my heels for brakes. One of these slopes was so very steep as to be dangerous to any one but a good snowshoer. The sliding snowshoes rush down hill, and are the real delight of that form of exercise, and are full recompense to those who can make them properly for the long, slow, heavy-breathing ascents of the summits.*[14]

This is likely the first ski mountaineering odyssey over this route and the first recorded account of a ski trek through the backcountry from Lake Tahoe to Donner Summit. It is possible that other local pioneers like McNutt, who skied throughout the winter, made this and similar trips, but this was the first published account describing the terrain and conditions the group encountered.

John Muir is best known for his summer rambles throughout the Sierra, but he was also a capable skier. He visited Lake Tahoe in early 1900, writing, "I have just returned from a week of bracing weathering around Lake Tahoe, in which we enjoyed glorious views of winter, fine rolling and sliding in the snow, swimming in the icy lake, and lusty reviving exercise on snow-shoes that kept our pulses dancing right merrily."[15]

Muir went on to detail the marked decrease in activity once winter arrived at the lake:

> *But winter brings rest. At sight of the first snowflake pleasure-seekers flee as from a plague, the ax leaves the woods, and the kind snow heals every scar.... Like the bears, the few settlers that remain here are silently "holed up." The snow covers their cabins as if they were bowlders* [sic], *and when approached only a narrow shoveled-out passage, or tunnel, is found leading to the door....A trapper may also be seen now and then shuffling along the shore on long Norwegian snow-shoes in pursuit of minks, fishers, and otters.*[16]

Muir and his companions spent a few days on the west shore of the lake at McKinney's. He wrote,

> *Here we spent a few health-giving, delightful days, rowing, bathing, racing at lightning speed on snow-shoes down a mountain-side back of the house, and slipping about through solemn, silent woods. Only the eldest of my companions ventured with me on the steep slopes. This was his first experience on snow-shoes, and the several descents he made were the most remarkable specimens of falling locomotion that I ever had the fortune to witness. In shooting down steep declivities the long sled-runner-like shoes have to be kept parallel with firmly braced limbs. My friend, however, heedless of advice, launched himself in wild abandon, bouncing and diving, his limbs and shoes in chaotic entanglement, now in the snow, now in the air, whirling over and over in giddy rolls and somersaults that would shame the most extravagant performances of the circus acrobat. How original and inimitable he was! Wonderfully refreshing and exhilarating his queer capers must have been; for on coming to rest, with his runaway members divorced and lost, he would quietly gather himself, pick out the snow from his neck and ears, and say with preternatural solemnity, "This, Muir, is the very poetry of motion."*[17]

Another turn-of-the-century winter visitor to Tahoe was photographer Arthur C. Pillsbury. Pillsbury's trip took place in early 1902, and his goal was to photograph the snowy landscapes of the High Sierra. His written and pictorial impressions of a Tahoe winter were published in the April 1902 issue of *Camera Craft* magazine.

Pillsbury went by train to Truckee, where he then disembarked and went by horse-drawn sleigh to the recently opened Tahoe Tavern. Winter visitors were few and far between, and he wrote, "At the hotel I met a warm welcome not unmixed with surprise. Visitors to Tahoe in the dead of winter are not numerous, and host and attendants talked with me as if a visitor from an outside world. Still, it was pleasant, and when I told them that I came to make pictures of the snow their interest increased."[18]

During a three-day snowstorm, Pillsbury spent time in the carpenter's shop making a sled for his camera and, under the instruction of the carpenter, crafted a pair of skis out of oak. He commented, "It was a job that I was proud of, for a lighter pair and a more serviceable one was not to be found in the whole of the Sierras."[19] However, he discovered that learning to use his new skis was quite challenging:

> *The skies* [sic] *I made were about eight feet in length, but before I was a finished performer I thought they were a hundred. After I learned the peculiar sliding motion indulged in by the natives I began to get along better. In a short time I was an expert and managed to keep abreast of the youngsters who served as my instructors. On level snow it is an easy operation. You shuffle along at an ordinary walking gait. The stride takes you about three feet, then you slide about a foot. Down hill you simply let go, then greased lightening couldn't catch you. Up-hill going consists of a series of tacks, much in the manner of a wind-jammer caught in the teeth of a gale.*[20]

Once the storm subsided, Pillsbury was able to put his handcrafted skis to the test. He, along with a group from the tavern, set out with his camera and portable darkroom in tow. His trip was a photographic success, and he prophetically noted, "Some day the Southern Pacific will run winter excursions to the lake, and the hotels will keep open all winter. Then the city man who wants to get out of the world for a few days will have the pleasures that I have merely hinted at."[21]

James E. Church, University of Nevada–Reno snow scientist, made many winter excursions in and around Lake Tahoe for his research. In 1915, he described his impressions of winter at the lake: "Lake Tahoe is

Photographer Arthur C. Pillsbury traveled to Lake Tahoe in winter 1902 to capture the beauty of the snow-covered landscape. *Courtesy of Melinda Pillsbury-Foster.*

an ideal winter resort for the red-blooded; for the viking and the near viking; for the man and the woman, who for the very exhilaration of it, seek the bracing air and the snow-clad forests. Lake Tahoe is as charming in winter as in summer, and far grander."[22]

James E. Church, professor of classics at the University of Nevada–Reno, was a pioneer in snow surveying, creating instruments and techniques that are still in use today. *Author's collection.*

Church also proclaimed that Lake Tahoe was perfectly suited for winter sports: "First, it is easily accessible; second, no place in the Sierra Nevada, not even Yosemite excepted, offers so many attractions; third, it is the natural and easy gateway in winter to the remote fastnesses of the northern Sierra."[23]

For Church, who was in nearby Reno, travel to the lake was relatively uncomplicated, but longtime Sierra Club member Lewis Clark wrote of the difficulty encountered by tourists journeying to the area in winter: "By 1915 Lake Tahoe had become known as a winter resort, with skiing of a sort as the chief mode of locomotion, but the ten-hour train trip to get there from the coast was discouragingly long and expensive."[24]

Ski trails wound through the forests at Tahoe City and other resorts that dotted the lake. Inns at Tahoe City and Glenbrook, the Grove near Tallac and the lodges at Fallen Leaf Lake remained open in winter and provided comfortable lodging for stalwart winter visitors. Skiers could ski from Truckee to the lake in one day if they traveled light. Or they could carry blankets and food by backpack or toboggan and overnight at Uncle Billy's, the halfway station. From November to April, sleigh service was available three times a week from Carson City to Glenbrook and from Truckee to Tahoe City. Travelers could then go from mail boat to train on Tuesdays and Saturdays.

Early Lake Tahoe residents utilized skis to hunt, trap and travel during the winter months, while winter tourists sought the beauty and solitude of the season. The next chapter illustrates how a group of early twentieth-century adventurers traveled into the mountainous backcountry, exploring and advocating for the pleasures that skiing can bring.

2

THE SIERRA SKI CLUB

Of all the Northern California ski clubs, the Auburn Ski Club has drawn the most attention and praise for promoting skiing in the 1930s. This recognition is well deserved, given the club's efforts and achievements to grow the sport when skiing was still in its infancy in California. But long before its founding in 1929, a group that called itself the Sierra Ski Club began visiting and exploring the Donner Summit area in winter.[25]

Lincoln Hutchinson, founder of the club, was a professor of economics at the University of California–Berkeley. He also served as financial advisor to the government of Czechoslovakia after World War II and was also involved in relief work in Russia. He learned to ski in Switzerland and then introduced the sport to his friends, many of whom were also professors at Berkeley. They began visiting Donner Summit in 1913. The only lodging available at that time was the Summit Hotel. But after it was destroyed by fire in 1924, the group experimented with ski trips to Cisco and Hobart Mills in hopes of finding ski terrain, along with lodging, that could match that at the summit. They concluded that the best skiing was on Donner Summit and the only way to be sure of comfortable lodging was to build their own lodge at Norden. The group formally organized the Sierra Ski Club in 1925 and built "the pioneer ski lodge in California."[26]

Once the decision was made to build the lodge, the group set out to find an ideal location and property that the club could purchase. Longtime Sierra Club member Harold Bradley described the club's land purchase at Norden:

Left: Lincoln Hutchinson was the founder and leader of the Sierra Ski Club from its beginnings in 1925 until his death in 1940. *Courtesy of Stanford University, American Relief Administration Russian operational records, Box 395, Envelope A, Hoover Institution Archives.*

Below: In the early 1920s, Summit Hotel was the only lodging on Donner Summit. When it burned in 1924, the few winter tourists who visited the area were left to stay in railroad sheds. *Donner Summit Historical Society, Norm Sayler Collection.*

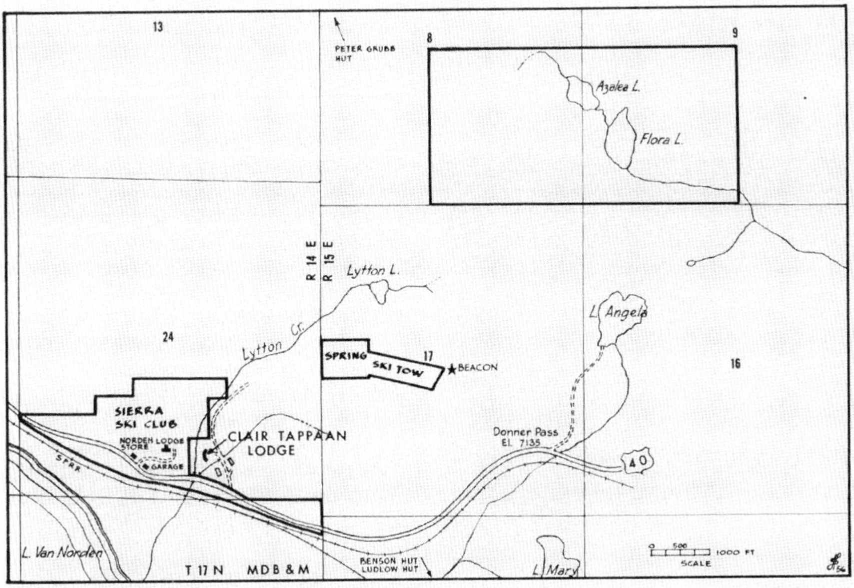

SIERRA CLUB PROPERTY AT NORDEN *Map by John P. Schagen*

Map showing the parcel of land the Sierra Ski Club purchased for their hut. Note also the location of Clair Tappaan Lodge and the Signal Hill ski tow. *Author's collection.*

> *They recognized the recreational potentialities of skiing in the Sierra, and fixed upon Norden as a site for the venture since access to the top of the range was there provided by the Southern Pacific Railroad. They acquired a strategic parcel of land just west of Donner Summit, and close to Norden station—some 67 acres of gently sloping brush and forest quite unspoiled by developments. They* [Lincoln and James Hutchinson] *also infected a very considerable number of their friends with their own enthusiasm for the project and the Sierra Ski Club was born.*[27]

Club members met in Berkeley on June 22, 1925, to formulate plans for the first summer of construction. It was decided that the cost of the building would not exceed $125 per member. Architect Walter Ratcliff designed the lodge, described as "a steep-roofed, stone-walled affair with strength specifications approximately one hundred fifty times standard requirements."[28]

Work began in summer 1925. Professor Joseph LeConte laid out the foundation lines by transit method, and eager workers began on the walls. The club's attorneys, professors, businessmen and doctors tackled the arduous job: "The builders were faced with the task of carrying up to a height of eight feet or more, walls of personally escorted stone, four feet thick in the buttresses, and then of adding a timber roof with plate beams a foot square."[29]

The cost of the building was divided among its thirty members, who could pay with cash or pay with labor. A salary credit of two dollars per day was given each worker. The workday began at 7:30 a.m. and ended at 3:30 p.m. with a two-hour lunch. This was a six-hour workday, but the members figured when horsepower and altitude factors were figured in, it was the equivalent of seventeen hours or more.

With the bulk of the work left for the following summer, the club was anxious to plan work party weekends, arranging for a meeting at Joseph LeConte's home on March 19, 1926. At this meeting, new ski club members were welcomed, a report on last summer's progress was given and preliminary work plans were drafted for the upcoming summer. Their motto for the summer was "Finish It or Bust!"[30]

All labor for the construction of Hutchinson Lodge was provided by club members on work party weekends. *Author's collection.*

Sierra Ski Club members take a well-deserved break as their ski lodge begins to take shape. *Author's collection.*

During the first summer, worker attendance was erratic and overhead costs high. To remedy this, Hutchinson formulated how many workers were coming and for how long. He estimated that a continuous group of eight workers for thirty days would get the lodge finished. With that plan and the dedicated labor of members, their ski house was finished by the end of summer 1926, at a total cost of $5,100.

The club published a 1926 *Sierra Ski Club Winter Bulletin* announcing the completion of the lodge. This was an historic first. It was the first club-built ski hut to be constructed in California and was a forerunner to the other winter lodges that the Sierra Club would build in the mountains throughout California.

The lodge provided skiers with shelter, hot and cold water, heat and a shower/bath. Members were responsible for their own bedding. The initial use of the hut was considered an experiment, likening it to an indoor camping trip.

Over the years, the lodge was used in both winter and summer and remained popular through the mid-1950s. Club membership varied from thirty to fifty members and was a virtual who's who of pioneer Sierra Club

Sierra Ski Club members celebrate the completion of Hutchinson Lodge. The club now had the much-needed winter lodging at their favorite ski grounds, Donner Summit. *Author's collection.*

members: William E. Colby, Joseph LeConte, Duncan McDuffie, Walter A. Starr, Harold C. Bradley and Joel H. Hildebrand.

Hildebrand, describing the Sierra Ski Club members, wrote,

> *The members were men in middle life from professional, business, and academic circles. They did not take their skiing too seriously, but they did discover that ski afford access to the mountains in their greatest beauty; and, including as they did a number of men influential in the nation-wide Sierra Club, they played a part in awakening that great organization to winter as well as summer mountaineering.*[31]

Hildebrand, a University of California–Berkeley professor of chemistry, discovered skiing through the Sierra Ski Club. He recounted some of his early experiences with the group:

> *We had a lot of fun. We would go up to this lodge* [Hutchinson Lodge] *between Christmas and New Years. Some of the members would walk*

Heavy snows surrounded the lodge during its first winter. *Author's collection.*

> *around on snowshoes; others would try to go on skis. Well, it was just what I wanted, because I loved the mountains in summer and to be able to go up in winter was also fun. You could not buy decent skis then. Spiro's in San Francisco sold skis, but they were likely to be jumping skis. But I read books, and I worked at it and gained some little skill.*[32]

Harold Bradley recalled the camaraderie among the club members:

> *The club, then, in its later years was a group of lifelong friends, who sought the seclusion of the Lodge for some days or weeks in winter—and also summer—for a care-free convivial period of relaxation. They loved each other. There was a wealth of wit and intellectual quality in the group, and no rules to govern debate or repartee.... Toward the end of such a restful day, the officer of the day would mix a potent libation. As the sun was setting Lincoln Hutchinson—and later Jimmy his brother—would ring a cow bell and call the group together. Leading the ceremony Lincoln would raise his glass; signal; and everyone present would yell "Sun—Set!" and dispose of the contents of the glass.*[33]

Lincoln Hutchinson died in 1940, but the club continued on under the leadership of his brother James until 1950, the last year the lodge was open during the summer. By this time, James was eighty-three years old, and he realized that the club was not gaining new younger members. The club's membership was aging and diminishing due to the death of many of the longtime members. The avid sportsmen who built the lodge and explored the mountains around the area in both winter and summer were elderly. At a Sierra Ski Club meeting held on May 12, 1955, members discussed transferring the ski club property to the Sierra Club. Further discussion took place in September, where some of the members executed deeds to the Sierra Club that night. The complete transfer of Sierra Ski Club grounds was complete by the end of 1955.

The minutes of a 1955 meeting of the Clair Tappaan Lodge Committee reported on the transfer process:

> *The property consists of a stone lodge and 75 acres around the Norden store area and including part of the town of Norden. The property has been offered to the Sierra Club. A committee was formed of Sierra Ski Club members to dispose of the property. The committee voted to recommend a gift of the individual shares to the Sierra Club. Almost all of the members and heirs have approved, provided the Sierra Club fulfill certain obligations. It becomes the responsibility of the Clair Tappaan Lodge Committee to administer the property and lodge.*[34]

Two of those obligations were for the Sierra Club to pay $275 to any Sierra Ski Club member who did not wish to make a gift of their interest in the club. And the Sierra Club agreed to pay James Hutchinson the amount the Sierra Ski Club owed him, which was approximately $5,000.

Harold Bradley later described the central role that Lincoln Hutchinson played in the club until his death:

> *As I have indicated, this was a group of warmly devoted friends. They were a highly talented group. Many were on the faculty at the U.C. or Stanford—though this was not a dominating group. Many were friends in college between 1890 and 1910. The idea of building a lodge and using it for skiing was Lincoln Hutchinson's, and he was the recognized leader as long as he lived. The Club was really forged by Lincoln. Later Jimmy took his place. Most of its quaint customs were introduced by Lincoln and Jimmy, Joe LeConte, Duncan McDuffie.*[35]

Ninety-four-year-old Hutchinson Lodge as it looks today, a living testament to the fortitude of the Sierra Ski Club. *Author's collection.*

The Sierra Ski Club lodge, eventually named Hutchinson Lodge after its founder, still stands today. Once Clair Tappaan Lodge was built in 1934, it became the lodge of choice for Sierra Club skiers. Hutchinson Lodge is still owned and operated by the Sierra Club for group lodging. The historic ski lodge represents the desire, skill and tenacity that Sierra Ski Club members possessed to conceive and build a shelter in order to indulge in their favorite winter pastime—skiing.

3
THE SIERRA CLUB ON SKIS

After decades of promoting California as the land of sunshine and flowers, the California State Chamber of Commerce eventually realized that winter sports would bring much-needed winter revenue to businesses that were normally shuttered in the winter. Along with the chamber, three other organizations played a part in awakening Californians to the prime ski fields right in their own backyard: the California Ski Association, founded in 1930, the Auburn Ski Club led by Wendell Robie and the Sierra Club. The enthusiasm and dedication of early Sierra Club skiers to the sport was described in a 1936 magazine article: "For several years these sturdy souls took the Southern Pacific night trains out of Oakland on Friday, dropped off at Cisco, slept in abandoned stations or out on the snows, skied two full days, then returned Sunday night fresh as daisies and ready for the grind of business. That shows what kind of stuff the Sierra Club is made of."[36]

There are only a handful of published sources of early twentieth-century ski excursions into the Tahoe and Donner area, but even these early skiers recognized the ideal ski terrain and climate that would eventually result in the region becoming a hotbed for skiers. Sierra Club members were some of the first to advocate for skiing on Donner Summit and surrounding mountains.

The Sierra Club organized one of its first winter sports trips in 1913. The participants traveled to Truckee by train and slept and ate in Pullman cars parked on a siding. This made it convenient for members to explore nearby hills on snowshoes and skis. A similar trip was made in 1914, with a thorough report of the trip written by Dr. Norman D. Kelley and published in the December 1914 issue of *California Out-of-Doors*.

Kelley wrote that many in the Sierra Club party practiced on skis, with some quite proficient and even two women taking the high jump with local expert ski jumper Irving Klepp. Many of the members were enthralled by the sport. It was decided that

> *with this winter's outing we are going to make skiing the main feature and encourage everyone to master it, best we advise those who wish to make the most of this sport to get their own skis and keep them from year to year.... From the mountaineering standpoint it is well for all Sierra Club members to be familiar with this way of getting around in the mountains....So let us all take the greatest interest possible in the ski and snowshoe.*[37]

Kelley was no doubt the first to envision the value of a ski shelter near popular ski grounds. He suggested that the Sierra Club build a structure near Truckee or Donner Summit to accommodate small parties of its members on the weekends and to store winter gear. He proposed a "good weather-tight shack, with two dormitories, a kitchen and lounging room with, of course, a huge fireplace and lots of wood, will fill the bill at first. This could be built or bought for inside $500."[38] Kelley's prophetic vision would be realized when the Sierra Club built Clair Tappaan Lodge in 1934.

As early as 1896, it was noted that "many of Truckee's woodmen can leap over precipices and fly down the steepest mountains."[39] It is likely these skiers were adept at straight running on their long skis but possessed little knowledge of turning techniques. When Sierra Club member Dr. Otto Barkan and Dr. Leo Eloesser visited Donner Summit during the winter of 1919–20, the railroad men who watched the pair saw that "it was possible to turn, swerve, or to stop, at a speed of forty miles an hour and over, avoiding obstacles, shooting between and around trees, in a glorious flying descent of perfect control."[40]

The Truckee men were rugged skiers when it came to long distances and extreme weather, but they had never seen such turns and control on skis. After spying the visitors' skis and bindings, the men soon emerged from their cabins with their newly remodeled skis and were soon imitating the telemark and Christiania turns they had watched with envy.

Barkan had visited the Swiss Alps, where he learned the alpine turning techniques prevalent in Europe at the time. In 1921, he and his Swedish wife, Margit, skied from Mount Lincoln to Mount Anderson and Tinker

Margit and Otto Barkan made numerous ski trips into the backcountry around Lake Tahoe in the 1920s. *Author's collection.*

Knob, glimpsing a view of Lake Tahoe, setting in motion a dream to ski to Tahoe across the mountains. This 1921 visit was the start of three winters at Donner Summit for Barkan and his companions. Dr. Duncan Morrison of Edinburg and Switzerland was part of that group, and alpinist Dr. Hans Lauper joined them in 1923. The group skied at Cisco, Truckee and Tahoe, but Barkan noted that "we always returned to Summit because of its better snow conditions."[41]

Barkan continued to frequent the summit over the years, and in 1927, he and his wife, along with friend Scott Smith, set out to fulfill their dream of crossing the mountains from Donner Summit to Lake Tahoe. The trip took fifteen hours, including one half hour reconnoitering and a half hour for rest. He estimated they covered between thirty and thirty-five miles. They reached the Tahoe basin as night fell. By this time, very tired and hungry, they skied along for two more hours from the Truckee River to Tahoe, where they recovered and thawed in a Pullman car.

On another outing in January 1929, Barkan and his wife spent a week exploring the terrain above Fallen Leaf Lake. They skied to Lakes Angora, Lucille, Heather and Desolation and spent fifteen minutes on top of windy, icy Mount Tallac. Of their descent, Barkan wrote, "The descent along the long southwestern slope of Tallac, where the wind-blown trees were coated with ice and there were no speed laws, was a grand experience."[42] This could very well be the first ski descent of Mount Tallac.

When Barkan and Eloesser visited Donner Summit in 1919–20, ski mountaineering was virtually nonexistent in California. In a few short years, the Sierra Club spearheaded the movement to encourage members to experience backcountry touring, not only around Tahoe and Donner but also throughout the state.

In the early 1930s, it seemed all of California became aware of skiing, especially after the National Ski Tournament was held at Lake Tahoe in 1932. The focus of skiing at that time was on ski jumping, with more people spectating rather than skiing. But ski participation would increase soon. In 1933, Lewis Clark wrote of the eventual transition from spectator-driven ski jumping exhibitions to ski touring and down-mountain skiing: "From state's end to end small groups and larger ones are preparing to go skiing, not merely to watch others. The majority are interested in ski-running and cross-country touring, but amateur racing and, to a less extent, jumping are attracting many devotees."[43]

Since the Sierra Club had been a leader in California hiking and mountaineering, many felt it only natural that it would lead the way in ski mountaineering and winter exploration of the mountains. David Brower, longtime executive director of the Sierra Club, noted, "As access to the snowbound Sierra became more practicable it was to be expected that the Sierra Club should lead in the encouragement of mountain touring in winter."[44] And Francis Farquhar wrote, "Every Sierra peak will before long have its first winter-ascent, and with these climbs will come new experiences, new triumphs over difficulties, new unfoldment of the grandeur and beauty of our High Sierra."[45]

In 1929, the Sierra Club formed its first Snow Sports Committee. This was the same year that the California State Chamber of Commerce formed its Winter Sports Committee. These were the first two California organizations to create a committee dedicated to furthering the cause of winter sports. The December 1929 *Sierra Club Bulletin* reported that the board of directors passed a motion that "a committee be appointed to encourage among members of the club the use of the High Sierra for winter sports."[46] The committee collected and disseminated information on snow conditions, weather and ski locations throughout the Sierra. It was made up of twenty-one accomplished skiers who would go on to make historic ascents and winter treks all over California. Eight of the members were based in Southern California. University of California–Los Angeles professor Walter Mosauer would go on to establish the Southern California Ski Mountaineers section of the Sierra Club in 1934. After meeting in December 1930, they recommended that the Sierra Club "enter into a program for the encouragement of winter trips and expeditions into the Sierra Nevada backcountry" and leave the development of resorts to others.[47]

The California Ski Association was primarily interested in promoting and sanctioning club and state ski tournaments, so their focus was on competition. The Sierra Club Snow Sports Committee's mission was to grow and provide opportunities for ski touring and ski mountaineering. To those ends, they published a *Snow Sports Manual* in 1933. The thirteen-page booklet, subsidized by the Southern Pacific Company, discussed equipment and clothing, included skiing literature and devoted four and a half pages to the mystery of waxing. Also advertised were the scheduled Sierra Club trips for early 1933 and the fares for Southern Pacific excursions from San Francisco to snow areas ranging from Yosemite to Shasta.

The introduction explained,

> *The Sierra Club, the largest mountaineering organization on the Pacific Slope, after having investigated the possibilities for adequate development of snow sports in California, has come to the conclusion that the snow regions of this state offer opportunities for the development of snow sports equal to the best conditions in the eastern United States and in Europe.*[48]

By the early 1930s, ski participation had been increasing, and by 1933, the Sierra Crest had already been crossed a number of times in winter. Harold Bradley skied over Echo Summit, down to Lake Tahoe and along the Truckee River to Truckee during winter 1920–21. He traced much of

Snowshoe Thompson's historic mail route. As previously mentioned, Dr. Barkan's group skied about 33 miles from Donner Summit, over the Mount Lincoln saddle, to Lake Tahoe in 1927. In 1928–29, Orland Bartholomew spent fourteen weeks skiing from Cottonwood Pass to Yosemite Valley. He crossed thirteen passes and spent forty-one nights above ten thousand feet. On November 30, 1931, Auburn Ski Club member Otto Lirsch and Walter Durfee skied from the Donner Monument to Emigrant Gap, covering about 27 miles in ten and a half hours. They followed the historic route taken by the Donner Party. In March 1932, Dennis Jones and Milana Jank skied over Tioga Pass to Yosemite Valley. They covered 130 miles on this trek, but it involved more than skiing. To navigate through Lee Vining Canyon, they had to cut ice steps for more than one thousand feet while carrying their skis.

Lodging near popular ski fields was scarce, and Joel Hildebrand described the accommodations during a trip he and some other Sierra Club members made to Soda Springs in 1934:

> *We chartered a bus to take us to Soda Springs where the women slept in cabins and the men on the floor of the abandoned railroad station. We had a grand time. On the way home I said, "The Sierra Club has several mountain lodges for use in summer; I propose that we get it to sponsor the building of a ski lodge." We there and then formed a committee. Several of the directors of the Sierra Club were members of our Sierra Ski Club, so the old Sierra Ski Club helped the birth of the Clair Tappaan Lodge.*[49]

The idea for a ski lodge was hatched on that February 1934 trip. On the trip home, Hildebrand recalled, "No one slept, for there was too much to talk about: skiing technique, waxes, boots, equipment....The most serious question, however, was where to spend the night on future trips. The obvious answer was a ski-lodge, owned and operated by the Sierra Club, and the Clair Tappaan Memorial Lodge then and there became an air-castle."[50]

The club chose an ideal spot in proximity to the Sierra Ski Club hut. The many virtues of this location were its accessibility by the Southern Pacific or by car via Lincoln Highway; the post office, store and public garage at Norden; and reliable and abundant snowfall.

Sierra Club members throughout the state supported the project, and every weekend during spring and summer 1934 workers were digging, sawing, hammering and chopping, some spending their entire vacation so that the lodge could become a reality and be ready for the upcoming winter.

The spirit and camaraderie of club members to singlehandedly create their own ski lodge is conveyed by the following recollection:

> *The year 1934 was one of tremendous activity. Plans were made, benefits held, materials and tools bought, and a stream of enthusiastic workers commuted to and from Norden every week end until the snow fell, to complete the first unit of the lodge. Dedicated on December 31, 1934, Clair Tappaan Lodge had its first capacity load—60 members, some of whom slept on the wide window seats in the main lounge-cum dining room-cum drying room.*[51]

The lodge was an immediate success, and by the first part of its second season, winter attendance was quadruple that of the same period during the previous season. On most winter weekends, the lodge was full.

Clair Tappaan Lodge eventually grew to accommodate 150 people in dormitories with a few small "cubicles" for families. Sleeping quarters were outfitted with bunks and mattresses; guests brought their own sleeping bags or blankets, soap and towels. Meals were served in a large dining room that also served as a theater and game room. A large main lounge with a fireplace and library provided a space to relax and recover from a long day's skiing. The remainder of the lodge had a drying room for wet clothing, lockers and a ski repair and waxing room. The lodge operated on a nonprofit cooperative basis, so every visitor was expected to contribute to housekeeping chores. Visitors selected their duties, which took only a few minutes a day.

Four years after its construction, Clair Tappaan Lodge would have its own ski tow, one of the earliest on the summit. In a May 1938 meeting of the Sierra Club Board of Directors, the Winter Sports Committee and the Clair Tappaan Lodge Committee were given approval to construct a ski tow near the lodge. Johnny Ellis had installed a ski tow nearby at Lake Mary in March 1938. That would become the year of the tows on Donner Summit. Ellis had his tow at Lake Mary, the Sierra Club had its tow on Signal Hill, Charles Van Evera installed a J-bar on Beacon Hill and a J-bar was installed at Rainbow Tavern.

Ellis's involvement with the Sierra Club and his expertise in building tows likely influenced the Sierra Club to have its own tow, and he was instrumental in the club realizing that dream.

Ellis, a Dartmouth graduate and active skier in the Dartmouth Outing Club, knew that Donner Summit possessed first-rate ski terrain. Comparing it to slopes in the East, he wrote, "Enough to make every skier in New England—Dub to Durrance—envious."[52]

Right: Brochure featuring Clair Tappaan Lodge in winter. It has been the ski headquarters for Sierra Club skiers on Donner Summit for more than eighty-six years. *Author's collection.*

Below: Clair Tappaan Lodge as it looks today. *Author's collection.*

Johnny Ellis (*right*) was a pioneer ski tow builder, installing some of the first lifts at Donner Summit. He assisted the Sierra Club with the construction of the Signal Hill ski tow. *Courtesy of Donner Summit Historical Society, Norm Sayler Collection.*

He spent several months in 1935 and 1936 at Clair Tappaan Lodge working as a carpenter, cook and caretaker. He began exploring locations for ski tows and wrote,

> *During this period of a summer and winter at Norden I began to get pretty interested in getting a rope ski-tow going near Signal Hill, also in starting a Dartmouth Outing Club of Northern California, also in buying land south of the pass….As far as the ski tow went, I tried to put in an electric one and got enough money raised and spent to owe a few hundred dollars to twelve of my friends. Then I found out the electric power was inadequate and unsuitable for the installation I had planned.*[53]

Sierra Club members on Signal Hill, circa 1937. The clear, open slopes were ideally situated near Clair Tappaan Lodge, prompting the Sierra Club to build the Signal Hill ski tow in December 1938. *Courtesy of www.thehighsierra.org.*

His wife, Evelyn, recalled that Ellis was building big wooden wheels in the basement of Clair Tappaan Lodge that would drive his Lake Mary tow. Since his previous experiment with electric power failed, his rope tows were powered with "a Model 'A' Ford set on a platform up above the snow, with the two wheels on the rear axle covered with oak blocks grooved to carry rope."[54]

The weekend of December 10 was a work party weekend, and club members carried nearly six thousand pounds of rope to outfit their new ski tow. By the end of December 1938, the club had erected a 2,600-foot ski tow that carried skiers up the face of Signal Hill. Skiers could then descend the mountain in almost any direction to return to the lodge. Its construction was partly financed by the advance sale of tickets. The tow was claimed to be the longest rope tow in America, and Clair Tappaan Lodge was the only Sierra Club hut with its own ski tow. It was immediately popular with guests, and this popularity spurred the club to re-rig pars of the tow, reduce the obstruction of lines around the powerhouse and improve the operating controls for the 1939–40 season.

The Signal Hill ski tow stretched 2,600 feet, providing skiers with a variety of long, open slopes. *Author's collection.*

Longtime Sierra Club member Dr. Joel Hildebrand was one of the biggest proponents of skiing in the northern Sierra Nevada and wrote of the appeal of the mountains in winter:

> *The Sierra Club is in the process of making a number of notable discoveries: that its beloved Sierra is the Sierra Nevada, or snowy range, and must be sought by devoted pilgrims not only in July, but also in January, to be known in the fullness of its glory; that winter at high altitudes is not bitter, but is warm and friendly, for the thin air easily transmits the radiance of the sun to bare brown backs; that twelve feet of snow affords a smoother path than even a national park trail, and runs anywhere you wish to go; that the purple shadows of the trees and the pure rose of the alpenglow are colors as rich as those of columbine and heather; that the smooth folds of sparkling virgin snow, the glitter of icicles, and the living green of firs showing beneath their heavy white mantles—all constitute an enchanted world which can be entered by the magic of the ski.*[55]

David Brower later recalled the many contributions that Hildebrand made to skiing:

> *Consideration of growth of skiing in the club must include special mention of Dr. Joel Hildebrand, who in a comprehensive sense has fathered skiing in this region. A competent skier himself, father of four active skiers, ski teacher and coach, developer of ski tests and inventor of ski games, author of many articles on skiing, supporter of the winter sports program of the club, acknowledged across the nation as a leader in ski sport, Professor Hildebrand's widespread influence in encouraging members to learn how to ski and in maintaining high skiing standards can only be suggested.*[56]

Hildebrand, professor of chemistry at University of California–Berkeley, took a sabbatical in 1930–31 so that he and his four children could spend the winter in Europe and attend the famous Hannes Schneider ski school at St. Anton. He remarked that they returned from this trip with a strong foundation of the ski technique of the day. Upon their return, in spite of their minimal experience, they were regarded as experts and found themselves helping others learn and enjoy the sport. Hildebrand went on to coach the 1932 United States Olympic Ski Team and, in 1938–39, was appointed the California editor of the *American Ski Annual*.

He was also responsible for securing Bill and Fred Klein to teach at Clair Tappaan Lodge. The brothers immigrated to St. Louis from Germany in 1934, joining their father, who had immigrated in 1932. They had no intention of staying in St. Louis and, after seeing a ski article written by Hildebrand, sent a letter to him spelling out their experience and qualifications as ski instructors. As recounted by Wolfgang Lert and Morten Lund, "It was a well-timed note. Sierra Club members, at Hildebrand's urging, had built their own ski lodge in 1934 in Donner Pass. It was a two-story building with kitchen and dorm rooms for sixty. During its first year, 700 skiers registered at Clair Tappaan and, during the next 1,100, indicating a growing need for instruction."[57]

Hildebrand replied to the letter asking the brothers to send a letter of recommendation from Franz Frank, their ski teacher in Traisen, Austria. Upon receiving the letter, Hildebrand offered the Kleins the Clair Tappaan ski school franchise, including room, board and fifty cents a lesson.

The Klein Ski School opened in the winter of 1936, the first ski school on the summit. Skiing was still in its infancy in 1936, and two developments—the advent of ski tows and Europeans to teach skiers the art of skiing—led to the proliferation of ski areas and skiers who could navigate the lift-served slopes

Right: Joel Hildebrand made many contributions to skiing, not just to the Sierra Club, but to the advancement of skiing throughout California. *Courtesy of Janet Hildebrand.*

Below: Sierra Club skiers were some of the first to embrace winter in the Sierra and, through the efforts of ski instructors like Joel Hildebrand and Bill Klein, possessed the skills to establish California ski mountaineering. *Courtesy of www.thehighsierra.org.*

Joel Hildebrand hired Fred (*left*) and Bill Klein to teach skiing at Clair Tappaan Lodge. The Klein Ski School was the first on Donner Summit. *Courtesy of Janet Hildebrand.*

in the late 1930s. There were no ski tows at this time, so their ski lessons consisted of trips up Mount Lincoln and surrounding areas. Lert and Lund noted, "This was ski mountaineering, but it was also the prelude to resort skiing in Donner Pass."[58]

The Klein Ski School was immediately popular. The Kleins collaborated with the other ski schools on the summit, loaning instructors to lodges to teach beginners, while the more advanced skiers were taught at Clair Tappaan. By 1938, Klein ski instructors were teaching 100–150 skiers each weekend. According to Lert and Lund, "This put it into the front ranks of U.S. schools at the time. Clair Tappaan was in a class with the Eastern Slopes Ski School under Benno Rybizka at Jackson New Hampshire, Otto Schnieb's school at Dartmouth in Hanover, New Hampshire, and Hannes Schroll's school at Yosemite."[59]

It can safely be said that the Kleins introduced several thousand new skiers to the sport during their first three seasons. They continued to attract throngs of skiers until December 1941, when the United States declared war following the attack on Pearl Harbor. Fred and Bill served in the war, leaving Peter Picard to direct the ski school during the war years.

Left: The Klein Ski School introduced thousands of skiers to the sport and was undoubtedly one of California's finest ski schools at that time. *Author's collection.*

Below: Signal Hill ski tow ticket. Advance ticket sales helped fund the construction of the tow and some winters the tow brought in more revenue than Clair Tappaan Lodge. *Courtesy of Diana Homsey.*

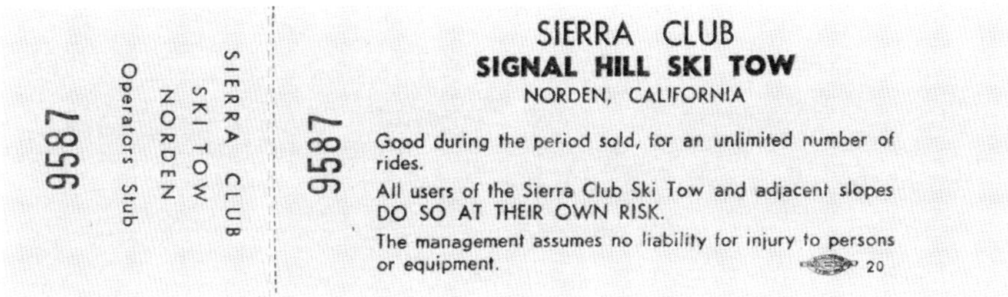

According to Picard, "After the Japanese attack on Pearl Harbor in December 1941, the U.S. military closed the road, which crossed the Southern Pacific rail bed, from Norden to Sugar Bowl. The idea was to prevent saboteurs from blowing up the rails. As a consequence of the road closing, Sugar Bowl had to shut down."[60]

Once Sugar Bowl closed, Clair Tappaan and its rope tow became the prime destination for San Francisco–area skiers for the next three winters. Lewis Clark, chairman of the Clair Tappaan Lodge Committee, described the importance of keeping the lodge open:

> *With our country at war, the Sierra Club must use its resources in the manner in which they may best aid the national defense. This means that until further notice Clair Tappaan Lodge will be operated as has already been planned, to provide recreational facilities for the members and to serve as a base for training of skiers in the ways of ski mountaineering and in the program of the National Ski Patrol. There will be more need than ever before for respite from the tensions of the city, and hence the Clair Tappaan Lodge Committee believes it is in the interest of civilian morale for us to continue, so far as possible, to operate the facilities as ski headquarters for our members.*[61]

Once the war was over, lodge activities eventually returned to normal. Work parties made improvements, Lewis Clark showed Sierra Club ski movies, and club leaders provided instruction on ski mountaineering, touring and safety.

In the 1950s, as surrounding ski areas expanded and skiers had the choice of many ski lifts in proximity to the lodge, use of the Signal Hill tow began to decline. In response, the Sierra Club began an aggressive publicity campaign promoting the warming room, hot drinks and other provisions available at the tow. Skiers responded, and tow receipts were responsible for most of Clair Tappaan Lodge's revenue during the 1950–51 season.

The tow underwent realignment in fall 1953, and the lodge committee reported that

> *the alignment of the rope was changed 20 degrees right which brought it close to being on our own property. Some clearing was done to enlarge the hill. The rope was run through the trees using the trees for a return, similar to before, which was fairly economical. The main cost was a new A-frame at the top, rebuilding the shives for alignment and the new rope. Left to do was construction on the shives, welding the A-frame, landscaping, and hanging the shives and rope.*[62]

The work on the tow paid off for the 1953–54 season. It was considered financially successful and brought in $2,200.

The tow was outfitted with a small warming hut, but by the mid-1950s it was decidedly too small and crowded. A new warming hut was completed for the 1955–56 season. Construction took place during the summer of 1955, but the need for the hut came about during the winter of 1953–54. Two very wet skiers were trying to get warm and dry in the old warming room, but space was limited and standing room only that day. They came to the same conclusion, that a larger space with more seating was needed. Architects George Homsey and Donn Weaver approached the Clair Tappaan Lodge Committee with the plan. Money was available from the operation of the ski tow, so they were given approval to design and supervise the building of a hut.

A committee was formed, made up of Homsey, Weaver, Bob Shepperd and Bob McGillicuddy (co-managers of the ski tow) and Bob McAndrews. As the project grew nearer, additional committee members were added to the roster: Art Benson, Don McCluskey, Don Huber, Jean Kearney, Sue Hart and Marie Gummerson. The committee was tasked with working out the construction, manpower and transportation schedule. The design was complete by summer 1954, and Homsey and Weaver created a model of the hut that was displayed

The Signal Hill tow house with the new A-frame on top. *Courtesy of Diana Homsey.*

at the lodge on New Year's Eve 1954–55. The model served to motivate members to contribute to the project and inspired more than one hundred members to work on the hut.

Homsey recalled the hard labor that went into building the hut:

> *The guys who were foresters cut down the lodge pole pine in the winter when the sap wasn't running. Then as soon as the snow melted, they dragged them out of the woods and brought the rock in. Then we started excavating and putting in the piers. Keith Lummis, the manager, got a bunch of timbers from the train sheds, probably 8 x 14s, twenty-five feet long, and we built a big false work. Then we laid the A-frames down on it, bolted them all together, and the guys climbed up in the tree with a rope and yanked them up.*[63]

The Signal Hill warming hut was just one of many mountain projects that George Homsey (1926–2019) designed and created. A prolific San Francisco architect, he was responsible for the design of the Clair Tappaan Lodge library and many of the other lodge additions over the years. He designed buildings

The Signal Hill warming hut under construction. The tow house is visible on the other side of the hut. *Courtesy of Diana Homsey.*

at Fallen Leaf Lake and several homes at Sea Ranch. He also created the Yosemite Design Guidelines that were adopted by the National Park Service. In 2006, he was awarded the Maybeck Award, the highest individual honor given by the California Council of the American Institute of Architects.

Bob McGillicuddy recalled that memorable summer of 1955:

> *The first work party began June 11–12 and the structure was essentially completed 20 weekends and approximately 600 man- and woman-days later. The high points of the construction were raising the first "A" frame, closing in the north wall, closing in the south end with windows, finishing the south rock wall, and building the first fire in the fireplace. The rock wall at the south end, supporting the windows, and the fireplace stack contain approximately 55 tons of rock and mortar.*[64]

Architect and Sierra Club member George Homsey, along with Donn Weaver, designed and spearheaded the construction of the Signal Hill warming hut. *Courtesy of Diana Homsey.*

Most of the rock was carried from within a half mile of the hut, but near the end of construction, a few select pieces of granite came from slides east of Donner Summit. The warming hut, in addition to the warming area with a fireplace, housed the tow motor and tow operator.

It is important to note the other members who accounted for four hundred of the six hundred work days, showing the truly team effort that became a hallmark of Sierra Club hut construction: Bob Crandall, Louise Dunlap, Alex Dzoghi, Bob Frick, Ray Helm, Don Huber, Stan Klein, Eric Kirschner, Anne and Peggy Kjellstrand, Dan Lee, Marian McDonald, Jim Mulholland, Tracy Norton, Jim Nicklos, Herb Rubin, Don Rehbein, Frank Shoemaker and Hank Schwarz.

As it had in the 1950s, the tow once again was struggling to survive against competition from nearby resorts. During the 1963–64 season, it was reported,

> *The ski tow was something of a disappointment. Even with high patronage at the lodge, relative trouble-free operation of the tow, good snow conditions, interesting competitive events, and excellent ski instruction, the income was down 25% from what should have been expected. The decline may be attributed to such factors as a package deal at Sugar Bowl to include Magic*

George Homsey's and Donn Weaver's design, with its A-frame and large windows, captured the spirit and character of California mountain architecture. *Courtesy of Diana Homsey.*

> *Carpet transportation with ski lift tickets, the need for our skiers to walk five-eighths mile to the ski tow, and perhaps to more affluence or skiing skill on the part of an increasing number of our members.*[65]

The competition from Donner Summit's larger, more established areas eventually led to the demise of the Signal Hill lift. After more than forty years of operation, the Sierra Club stopped running the historic tow in 1979 and it was removed sometime thereafter. The warming hut continued to be used until 2004, when it was finally closed due to a rodent problem. Clair Tappaan Lodge continues to be owned and managed by the Sierra Club. Lodging is available for members and non-members, and even though the Signal Hill tow no longer operates, skiers have close access to the slopes at Boreal Mountain, Donner Ski Ranch, Sugar Bowl and Soda Springs.

The warming hut still stands on land that is now part of the Truckee Donner Land Trust and is a testament to the talent and dedication of George Homsey, Donn Weaver and the other Sierra Club members who volunteered their time and labor to improve the historic Signal Hill rope tow area.

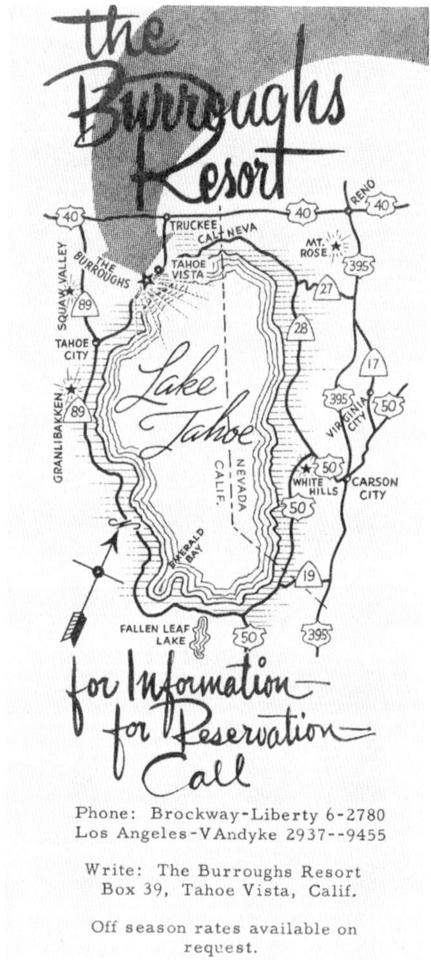

Burroughs Resort brochure and map. It was the only privately owned lodge at North Lake Tahoe outfitted with a ski tow. *Author's collection.*

4

NORTH LAKE TAHOE

Burroughs Resort

The Burroughs Resort was a privately owned year-round lodge located on the north shore of Lake Tahoe at Tahoe Vista. It operated a rope tow for guests, proclaiming, "Burroughs Resort is midway of Squaw Valley and White Hills, 8 miles from Olympic Hill, and Granlibakken Ski Fields—and with a 750-foot rope tow and ski run right in our own backyard, it's no wonder Burroughs Resort is a favorite."[66]

The resort catered to ski groups, and since it was located only eight miles north of Tahoe City, it also supported the Tahoe-Truckee Unified School District's ski school program.

The resort was named for its first owner, Mack Burroughs. He then sold it to Gerald and Pricilla Potts in the early 1950s, who owned it into the early 1970s. The rope tow operated in the 1950s, but it is unknown when it ceased operation. The Burroughs, along with other North Lake Tahoe resorts, provided skiers with many lift-served ski areas to choose from.

The rope tow at Burroughs Resort was a real convenience for families with young children and youth groups. Once at the resort, they had lift served skiing right outside their door. *Author's collection.*

TAHOE CITY–LAKE TAHOE SKI CLUB

By the late 1920s, enthusiasm for skiing was growing rapidly, especially the crowd-pleasing and exciting ski jumping tournaments. This popularity resulted in a growing number of winter visitors making their way to the Tahoe and Donner areas, prompting the Tahoe Tavern to remain open in December 1926, the first time in its history that it was in business during winter months.

Jack Mathews, manager of the Tahoe Tavern and president of the Lake Tahoe Ski Club, realized that winter guests would appreciate having a jump nearby, rather than having to make the sometimes-difficult trek to Truckee, then the nearest jump to the tavern. The hill would not only serve winter guests but could also double as ski grounds for the club. So, in July 1929, Tahoe Tavern contributed $3,000 toward the construction of a ski jump. In August, Mathews hired champion ski jumper and ski jump designer Lars Haugen to build it.

The jump was finished in December 1929, and it became the site of many major ski meets throughout the 1930s. In its first three winters, the hill was home to California's first significant ski jumping tournaments. In February 1930, the newly christened jump was the site of the state's first major ski meet. Then, on February 21–22, 1931, the California division tryouts for the 1932 Winter Olympics were held. And completing the trifecta was the February 1932 national championships. Eventually known as Olympic Hill, it was situated about twelve miles from Truckee and about two miles from Tahoe City. It was located where today's Granlibakken Resort still operates.

Over the years, the Lake Tahoe Ski Club held many of its club tournaments there. But, by the 1938–39 season, club members were hoping to have their own area rather than make costly improvements to the slopes at Olympic Hill. At a meeting held on November 18, 1938, the club voted unanimously to purchase sixty-eight acres at a cost of $800 for their winter sports grounds. The land was located in Tahoe City just off the main highway, above the golf course, behind what is currently Save Mart. The club planned to build a new ski jump, toboggan slide and downhill and slalom courses served by a ski tow. The new location did have limitations as a jumping venue, but the proximity of the new location to Tahoe City outweighed any concerns about the new jumping hill: "Members are willing to admit that while longer record jumps can be made from Tahoe's famous Olympic Hill in Ski Canyon, access is difficult and painful to many who are unseasoned winter sportsters."[67]

Members were committed: they raised $1,400 through a membership drive, donations and a loan. The deal was completed on November 28, and the club immediately set to work. They cleared a 200-foot-wide by 1,400-foot-long slope where downhill and slalom races could be held.

In addition to clearing the main slope, members constructed a new warming hut that was ready for use by Christmas. Local businessmen generously contributed to the project: N.R. Mayfield donated lumber, materials and money, and Carl Bechdolt Sr. contributed the tin roof and wood-burning stove. The one-thousand-foot rope tow was installed and ready for its debut in early January 1939. Ski jumping champion and Lake Tahoe Ski Club member Sig Ulland worked on the hill, and Joe Henry, auto mechanic, tournament director and ski jumping judge, installed the gas engine for the ski tow. Club president Carl Bechdolt Jr. helped clear trees and oversaw other improvements. For jumping events, the club continued to use Olympic Hill until it could build a jump at the new location.

The club held its first meet at the Tahoe City hill on Sunday, February 5, 1939. Slalom and downhill races were held, along with a jumping meet that was held on a temporary jump. Attendance at the meet was estimated at less than fifty skiers, with out-of-town competitors deterred by the threat of poor weather.

The new hill was popular with local and visiting skiers, and by the close of the 1938–39 season, the club was planning to make needed improvements during the summer months and began working on the upgrades in earnest. Contractor C.T. Thomas and his crew removed trees and shrubs, clearing a larger area for the ski jump and slalom course. The ski tow was lengthened and a more powerful motor installed. At a ski club meeting on November 10, 1939, ski hill improvements were discussed, and any member who donated at least thirty hours of work on the grounds was awarded a season pass for the tow.

Later that November, Charles Swanson deployed more than three hundred pounds of explosives to blast away stumps for new runs and ski jumps. And in early December, the club was rushing to get the hill in shape before the season's first significant snowfall. Bob Watson was clearing obstructions and smoothing the hill with his tractor. A small house that was at the foot of the hill had been moved, and work was ongoing to lengthen and increase the power of the upski.

The Tahoe City hill may have been sufficient for the rope tow, but its location for a jump could not compare to Olympic Hill. At the November 10, 1939 meeting, it was reported, "After an inspection of the new ski hill

The Lake Tahoe Ski Club rope tow carried skiers to the top of the slope behind the golf course, visible at center right. *Courtesy of Bill Briner, photographer, and Carol Van Etten.*

earlier in the week, several members felt that the old Olympic hill might be preferable for jumping events in sanctioned meets this winter."[68] In spite of those concerns, in October 1940 the club went forward with developing a jump in Tahoe City. The *Sierra Sun* reported,

> *The Lake Tahoe Ski Club's new jumping hill at Tahoe City is progressing daily under the work of county crews, tractors and bulldozers which are clearing out bushes and rocks and levelling the slopes. The newly elected president A.M. Henry, with Director Carl Bechdolt, Jr., surveyed the work done on Sunday and made plans for construction of the landing apron which will be surveyed this week by John Burns. The hill will be large enough to make 150-foot jumps and will be used by Class A, B, C, and D jumpers. It will have two take-offs.*[69]

It is unknown how much this jump was utilized by Class A and B jumpers, but the club scheduled competitive events for both Tahoe City and Olympic Hill so that the jumping meets would not be hindered by an unsatisfactory hill.

Skiing activities were scaled back during the war but resumed in earnest thereafter. In January 1946, club members were elated when new rope for the club's hill arrived from the east. Club members went to work to get the new tow operating as soon as possible. And at a club meeting held on January 3, members agreed to lease the upski and food concession to Mr. and Mrs. James Goodhue. A season pass for the tow was $5.00, individual rides were $0.15 and an all-day ticket cost $1.50.

Maintenance and operation of the tow were genuine community efforts. Many club members donated significant time and money over the years to keep the tow in good working order and to continually make improvements to the hill. Businesses also made substantial contributions. Shell Oil Company donated one hundred gallons of gas during the 1945–46 season for the operation of the upski. And the Gardner brothers of Reno donated hill work for the 1946–47 season.

In fall 1946, the Tahoe City once again underwent extensive improvements. The *Sierra Sun* reported on the work that was taking place:

> *A bulldozer has been working at widening the present hill apron by 100 feet, removing rocks and trees, lengthening the landing and raising the takeoff. Carl Bechdolt, Sr., of Tahoe Inn, who owns land adjacent to the club's property, has agreed to remove trees from the lower end of his land and will fill in the marshy section with dirt, eliminating the soft spots which prevented use of the section at the base of the apron last season. Charles Swanson, one of the club's oldest members, on Monday dynamited a huge stump from the side of the hill and after all the work has been completed, Tahoe will possess one of the finest hills in the west.*[70]

The tow was also improved, with Bill Bechdolt, Pete Vanni and Floyd Carnell installing a new rope and Fred Main securing a new motor. The tow, formerly 1,200 feet long, now extended to 1,400 feet. Bechdolt spent $500 clearing his land for the club. But all of the other improvements that were made came at a cost of about $1,000 to the club.

The club continued to use the Tahoe City hill and in 1948 made additional improvements, including installing floodlights for night skiing. However, the rope tow had only a 200-foot rise, and new lifts and runs were not being added. In fall 1948, the club focused on improving the ski jump at Olympic Hill, and in fall 1949, plans were made to renovate the rope tow at Olympic Hill. The club continued to use the Tahoe City hill for cross-country events and some slalom races, but use of the ski tow came to an end, as club members preferred the greater variety of terrain available at Olympic Hill.

There was one last attempt to revive the hill in February 1958. Led by Dave McBride, the crew got the motor in place and spliced and strung the rope. Once the insurance was in place and a safety gate installed, the rope tow would be open for use by club members. McBride was assisted by Jim Williamson, Dinty Moore, Bill Bechdolt, Jack Starratt, Dick Clarke and Alan Lewis.

In December 1959, the *Sierra Sun* reported that the Lake Tahoe Ski Club had been reactivated and would be hosting the Squaw Valley Olympic Games, along with Sugar Bowl, Heavenly Valley and Reno Ski Clubs. So, as the club became involved in other activities and larger ski areas were developed around the lake, it may be that the club no longer wanted to shoulder the expense and extensive work it took to maintain, improve and operate its own tow.

The Lake Tahoe Ski Club's Tahoe City rope tow operated over a span of ten years, but by the 1950s, club-owned tows were becoming a thing of the past, while privately owned ski areas grew and supplanted the club-operated tows. And in 1948, nearby Squaw Valley constructed two chairlifts, likely enticing skiers away from the Tahoe City hill. The Lake Tahoe Ski Club still exists today and can celebrate the vital role it played in Lake Tahoe's ski history—developing skiers and hosting ski meets at both Olympic Hill and Tahoe City.

Powder Bowl–Deer Park

Powder Bowl Ski Area was located on Highway 89 just three and a half miles north of Tahoe City at the entrance to Alpine Meadows. Situated on the north side of Deer Park Mountain and North Scott Peak, the area first became known for tobogganing, snowshoeing and other winter sports activities that could last into June or July. Even in the late nineteenth century, there were some who felt that "there was no better location in the whole Tahoe area for a public recreation area than Deer Park."[71]

Jerry Waters, a Texan, moved to the Tahoe area in the late 1940s and, at the age of forty-seven, was taught to ski by Émile Allais. He and Allais surveyed the mountains around Deer Park as a possible ski area location. Then, in 1954, Waters was granted a Forest Service lease for 320 acres and the Deer Park Development Corporation was born. Dave Fritschi, vice president of the corporation, financed the expansion and development of the area.

In November 1957, Waters, who had been operating a couple of rope tows, anxiously awaited the arrival of his 2,600-foot-long Poma lift. In previous winters, Waters made trips into the nearby backcountry, scouting out additional terrain to the southwest of Deer Park Lodge. He found excellent terrain for all levels of skiers. He reported,

> *The lift is due in Deer Park about November 10, and weather permitting, should be completely installed by Thanksgiving weekend. If the gods of weather are fickle, it is a sure thing to be operating by Christmas. This lift, about 2600 feet long with a vertical rise of 1000 feet, opens up terrain that promises to be the finest for skiing. The complete northern exposure will insure the best snow conditions for the ability levels of all skiers.*[72]

Powder Bowl officially opened in December 1957 with its new Poma lift installed in time for Christmas. It offered free skiing on December 21 and held a Fun Race Day on December 26. The race was open to all children under ten years of age and consisted of "obstacle races coupled with not-too-serious slalom contests."[73]

The Poma lift ran to the top of Powder Peak, giving skiers a nine-hundred-foot vertical drop. It served a variety of runs for all levels of skiers and even had a beginner run for those who wanted a longer run than that provided by the rope tow. The lift could carry six hundred skiers per hour. Waters estimated the hill could handle about five hundred skiers and the parking lot about three hundred cars.

Improvements carried over into the second year of operation. A large day lodge, dubbed the Red Hut, was completed and outfitted with a kitchen, fireplace and lounge area. A shop adjacent to the Red Hut provided rental equipment, skier accessories and a repair shop. Lodging was provided nearby at Deer Park Lodge. Situated right on the Truckee River, managers Cal and Jean Calhoun operated the lodge, apartment and cabin facilities, accommodating up to 135 visitors. In December 1959, well-known ski instructor Eric Johnson became the ski school director, and the Powder Bowl Ski Club was formed in January 1960.

The year 1960 also marked the beginning of one of the wackiest and most popular races ever held in the Sierra, the Barrel Stave Olympics. Originated by Waters, it was described as "a combination roller derby, hockey match, [and]

Base area buildings, the Poma lift and ski trails are laid out in this vintage Powder Bowl map. *Author's collection.*

professional wresting bout."[74] The annual event was sponsored by the Powder Bowl Ski Club and Paul Masson Vineyards of San Francisco. Vineyard representatives were on hand on race day, brewing glogg wine for the spectators.

Two racers would leave the starting gate at the same time, and all manner of moves could be used to prevent the opposing skier from making it through the gates. Teams were made up of two men and one woman, and the team with the best total time was the winner. The top three teams and the three fastest individual skiers were awarded trophies—a miniature half-gallon Paul Masson wine keg.

The barrel stave skis were prepared and provided by the Powder Bowl Ski Club. The setup consisted of twenty-four-inch staves, a leather strap over the boot toe and a boot lace for a long-thong wrap. Two parallel courses were set so two racers could race side by side down the course. Another requirement was that racers were expected to wear crazy costumes, a virtual Halloween-like party on skis. Waters described what it was like to ski on barrel staves: "Skiing on Barrel Staves is something like riding a rocking horse and the best skiers don't necessarily win, but it's more fun than a barrel of monkeys and the spectators as well as the competitors will be in for an hilarious afternoon."[75]

In December 1961, Dick and JoAnne Austin purchased Powder Bowl. The acquisition included the restaurant, ski shop, ski school, two rope tows and a Poma lift. But nearby and larger Alpine Meadows opened in 1961, creating competition right at Powder Bowl's doorstep. And Squaw Valley and Granlibakken were less than a twenty-minute drive away.

By the mid-1960s, small ski areas were beginning to struggle to keep up with the larger areas. In 1966, Leigh Rovzar was managing Powder Bowl, and

Above: Eric Johnson, ski instructor, racer and commercial artist, popping the cork on Paul Masson champagne during Barrel Stave race festivities. *Author's collection.*

Opposite, top left: Ski writer Carson White catching air during a barrel stave race. *Author's collection.*

Opposite, top right: Powder Bowl was popular in its first few years, but Alpine Meadows presented serious competition when it opened in 1961. *Author's collection.*

Opposite, bottom: Eric Johnson (*right*) assists with the trophies for the 1961 barrel stave races. *Author's collection.*

for family fun!
SKI
POWDER
BOWL
FWSIA
Dick Austin
SKI SCHOOL
On Highway 89
At The Entrance
To
ALPINE MEADOWS

Paul Masson
BARREL STAVES
OLYMPIC SLALOM

he noted that smaller resorts have to expand to attract skiers, commenting, "We get the overflow from Alpine, but in order to get these same people back we have to stay competitive. We have to give them something in the way of skiing. Beginners are the chief breads and butter of small areas like ours. And we develop them for the larger areas."[76] So, the days of ski areas with a couple of old rope tows and a small day lodge were beginning to pass. It would take real money and expansion to save them.

Also, a number of Tahoe ski resorts, including Powder Bowl, were at a disadvantage and sometimes struggled because of their lower elevation. The winter of 1975–76 was a low snow year. Increased business in the ski school helped cash flow, but they were operating with a skeleton crew to keep their payroll at a minimum.

New owners took over the old Powder Bowl Ski Area in December 1980. Optimism ran high, and along with new ownership came a new name. Powder Bowl was renamed Deer Park Ski Area. President, majority shareholder and general manager Gerhard Stoll said, "Deer Park has, potentially, some of the best advanced and expert skiing in California."[77]

One of the biggest challenges the new owners faced was the limited parking. To remedy the problem, they proposed nearby off-site parking; skiers would then be transported to the area by shuttle bus. The three possibilities they examined were a location near Squaw Valley, a site near the highway junction at Tahoe City and a site one mile beyond Tahoe City at Dollar Hill. But, for the first three years, Deer Park planned to use a secluded parking lot near the entrance to Squaw Valley Road, providing a free shuttle bus to the ski area.

Stoll made extensive plans for the future of the resort. Once the master plan was realized, the area would cover 1,500 acres and be served by eight chairlifts and four surface lifts with a total vertical of 2,000 feet. The buildout would be complete by 1990, ending up with 20 percent beginner runs, 43 percent intermediate and 37 percent expert terrain. For comparison, when the area opened for the 1982–83 season, it had thirteen runs with 830 vertical feet on 218 acres. The longest run was one mile long.

The first phase of improvements stretched over two years, and Deer Park finally reopened for business for the 1982–83 season. During the busy fall, management cleared ski runs, repaved the parking lot, installed the footings for the lift towers, constructed a new and separate beginners' area served by two surface lifts and made some improvements to the lodge. It opened on Thanksgiving Day with three Poma lifts servicing the beginners' area, and once the chairlift began operating, it would open up advanced skiing terrain. The long-awaited triple chair had a capacity of 1,800 skiers per hour, but because of the small parking lot, only 500 skiers per day would be allowed on the slopes. The chairlift was finally delivered in December, so it did not begin operating until January.

Unfortunately, the remainder of the ambitious master plan for Deer Park was never completed. After only two seasons, there were financial problems that prevented the area from opening for the 1984-85 season. Prior to the 1983–84 season, management was being reorganized, and by the time positions were in place, a few key weekends had been missed. This led to fewer skier days than projected, and those skier days were necessary to make the area profitable. Deer Park filed for bankruptcy in December 1983, and the owners of the chairlift removed it in fall 1984 because they hadn't been paid. The bankruptcy was approved on November 19, 1984, and the area was then purchased by Alpine Meadows. Meadows management were only interested in using the Deer Park parking lot as a base for their shuttle buses and did not intend to revive it as a ski resort. Howard Carnell, Alpine Meadows president, noted, "We've made a pretty extensive study of Deer

View of the Deer Park base area today. The building on the left served as the lodge and cafeteria. The building on the right was used for ticket sales, rentals and the ski school. *Author's collection.*

Park and honestly don't see it as economically feasible to operate it as a ski area. I can't say what will happen down the road, but for now, we have no plans to develop it as a ski area."[78]

Leigh Rovzar, Deer Park's former manager and longtime investor, didn't agree with Carnell's assessment of the potential at Deer Park, especially since he had done extensive planning and felt the potential for a larger, viable ski area was there. Commenting on Deer Park's final seasons, he said, "There was some confusion about that time concerning who was going to do what and who was going to run the operation."[79] Rovzar also noted that of the final two years that Deer Park was open, neither was a full season.

Alpine Meadows still owns the acreage that was home to the Powder Bowl–Deer Park ski area. The base area buildings still stand and are being used as office space by Alpine Meadows. An old hand-painted Deer Park trail map still hangs on one of the walls. The former ski runs can still be seen, and rusty lift equipment litters the slopes. It survives as one of

Above: The old bullwheel and upper terminal of the Poma lift can still be found on the deserted slopes of Deer Park. *Author's collection.*

Opposite: Hand-painted Deer Park trail map still hangs on the wall in the former day lodge. *Author's collection.*

California's many lost ski areas, succumbing to the challenges of expansion and adequate revenue. It is evidence that small ski areas, without funds for expansion, snowmaking or other improvements, likely end up as another of California's lost ski areas.

PAPOOSE–SKI ANY MOUNTAIN

Wayne Poulsen spent most of his life involved in skiing, and his imprint on California skiing lingers even today. A student at the University of Nevada–Reno (UNR), Poulsen recalled his early years:

> *When I was still in school, I worked summers at Hobart Mill, which is a little north of Truckee. My friend Marty* [Arrouge] *and I used to go up to Tahoe City all the time. He had a Ford with a rumble seat. We'd go up the Truckee River Canyon and each time we passed the entrance to Squaw Valley, I would look back at the peak in the distance, but it was not until 1932 that I went into the valley and that was to go fishing. After that I went up there a lot and thought that it was a good place for a ski area, so in 1938 I took an option to buy land in the valley.*[80]

While at UNR, he organized the university's first ski team, serving as its captain and, after graduation, as coach. In 1937, he initiated the very popular University of Nevada Winter Carnival.

Poulsen excelled as a jumper, alpine skier and ski mountaineer, having spent two winters on the crest of the Sierra conducting snow surveys. There were a number of spectacular ski jumping exhibitions in the 1930s, and he participated in all of them: the Auburn Ski Club's jump at University of California–Berkeley in 1934 and 1935, the Lake Arrowhead Ski Club's jumping meet at the Los Angeles Coliseum in 1939 and the Treasure Island ski jump at the world's fair in San Francisco in 1939.

Ed Heath dubbed Poulsen the "Skimaster of Reno," and Heath vividly described Poulsen's early years: "Wayne Poulsen, first ski citizen of Nevada, took to the boards when he was a miniature curly-headed Viking of nine winters and has been hard at it ever since. He was a familiar sight in the early days of skiing, trailing around after the Mikkelsens, Haugens, and other Scandinavians in the Cisco-Donner Summit region who have made so much California ski history."[81]

Wayne Poulsen developed and operated four different ski areas over the years: Mt. Rose, Squaw Valley, Cisco Tunnel Mountain and Papoose. *Author's collection.*

Upon graduating from UNR, Poulsen earned his pilot's license. After a short stint in Canada with the Royal Canadian Air Force, he returned to the United States and began flying for Pan Am. By 1943, he had the money to purchase 640 acres in the west end of the valley. Poulsen met Alex Cushing in 1947, and the two became partners in the first lift and lodge to be built in the valley. In 1948, the Squaw Valley Ski Corporation constructed two chairlifts, and that same year Poulsen purchased additional acreage in the valley.

The saga of the contentious Poulsen-Cushing partnership and how Cushing promoted Squaw Valley as the 1960 Olympic venue has been told and retold. But in 1957 and 1958, when Olympic planners threatened to destroy the natural beauty of the valley, it was Poulsen and his wife, Sandy, who stood firm against the imminent destruction of the meadows and mountains. They were criticized from all sides, but they successfully fought and defeated plans for an asphalt parking lot, an open bed sewage plant and a four-lane highway around the valley.

Poulsen's first foray into operating a ski area was in 1938 when he started the development of Mt. Rose Ski Area. He installed tows, a restaurant and a ski shop. In 1940, he became an instructor and started his Ski School Tyrol on the slopes of Mount Rose. His expertise as a skier was readily passed on to students. His philosophy was that "only those students who completely master the fundamentals can become expert and graceful skiers. He insists that his

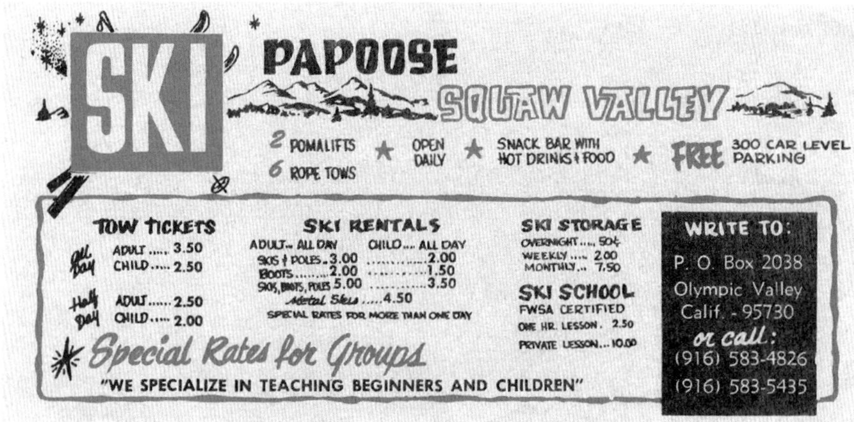

Papoose was the ideal area for beginners and families not yet ready to take on the more challenging terrain at Squaw Valley. *Author's collection.*

pupils become not mere elegant 'slope-dopes' but all-round skiers who can feel at home on and enjoy every variety of snow condition and terrain."[82]

Later, during the 1952–53 season, he opened a small enterprise called Papoose Ski Area in Squaw Valley. He would go on to own the area for almost thirty years, focusing on teaching families and beginners. In preparation for the 1958–59 season, he made many improvements to the area, installing a 1,200-foot-long Poma lift and adding snow making.

The area continued to grow over the years, and by the 1962–63 season, Papoose was operating six rope tows and two Poma lifts. Always a jumper at heart, Poulsen added a small jumping hill. The thirty-to-forty-meter jump included a judge's stand and a rope tow to serve the jump and the adjacent slalom course.

Poulsen and his wife, Sandy, catered to young skiers by creating special races. In 1966, they started the Santa Claus Slalom and Snow Bunny Slalom for kids up to nine years old. Papoose also hosted the Tahoe-Truckee Unified School District learn-to-ski program.

By the end of 1970, Papoose had five and a half acres of beginner slopes and specialized in teaching novices and children. Its reputation grew as a beginners' area; a 1973 article noted that it was "a good place to overcome initial fear of skiing—each run is progressively steeper."[83] The beginners' hill became the pride of Papoose, with management taking extra care to create one of the best slopes for beginners and junior skiers: "Consistency is the key word. The same grade all the way down is its outstanding feature. The hill is completely groomed at all times. Fresh powder is packed down and the hard ice crust is broken up and rolled to provide a good consistent skiing surface."[84]

Poulsen sold the area in 1981 to Bud Hoffman, owner of Any Mountain Ltd., a ski shop in Cupertino, California. Hoffman renamed it Ski Any Mountain after his ski shop. With fifteen acres of easy-to-moderate slopes served by three surface lifts, the area continued to tailor its services to the beginning and intermediate skier.

Sadly, Ski Any Mountain closed around 2000, ending almost fifty years of skiing history at that site. Then, in 2010, when KSL Capital Partners, a Denver private-equity fund, purchased Squaw Valley, Ski Any Mountain was never to open again. Its slopes were merged into those of Squaw Valley.

Poulsen began skiing when the sport was in its infancy in California. Commenting on those early days, he said, "When I was a kid, I had to make my own skis, shaping them in the steam from Reno Hot Springs. For Bogners, I wore an old pair of hand-me-down Tuxedo pants!"[85] Poulsen wore many hats over the years. He served as the first president of the Squaw Valley Development Company, formed with Cushing to build the first lift and lodge. He also headed the Squaw Valley Land and Livestock Company, developer of the valley community, which included a shopping center and post office, two churches, the Papoose Ski Area, restaurants, a lodge and residential lots. Over the years, he has also acted as surveyor, planner, lawyer and, most importantly, defender of his property and principles. Papoose was a small beginners' area but left a lasting effect on many who skied there. Wayne Poulsen Jr. summed up the influence that small family ski areas could have on young skiers: "You should be confident to know that the Papoose area is no mere cypher, but was a winter constant, a year to year reality for me every year from the early fifties until the late sixties, the entire time that I was growing up in Squaw."[86] Little Papoose Ski Area has been gone for many years, but the beauty of Squaw Valley stands as a living testament to Poulsen and his love for the valley that he first saw in 1932.

5
HIGHWAY 50

U.S. Highway 50, considered "America's Gateway to the West," began as a major corridor for gold seekers and migrants traveling to California.[87] Between 1850 and 1857, it was a rough and rocky trail. The discovery of the Comstock Silver Lode in Washoe Valley, Nevada, in 1859 led to throngs of travelers along the route. It became lined by saloons, bars, and gambling rooms and was often plagued by mud, ice, snow and avalanches. Some of these hazards continue to plague sections of the highway even today. With the advent of the automobile age, it evolved into one of the main cross-country routes and became California's first state highway in 1895.

The Tahoe area's terrain and climate are ideally suited for the makings of a winter sports mecca. But as western historian W. Jackson Turrentine wrote, "Since Tahoe had become a resort in the 1870s, winter meant hibernation."[88]

Harvey Gross of Harvey's Resort Hotel and Harvey's Inn understood the importance of highway snow removal to the advancement of winter recreation and commerce. Prior to the construction of the maintenance station built on Echo Summit at the south end of Lake Tahoe in September 1941, Tahoe was too inaccessible for winter visitors.

Gross recalled the efforts that locals made to prove to the governor that the road needed to be kept open:

> *That took a united effort of the community. The State never attempted to keep the road open. The governor at that time said it was impossible, and as soon as there was two feet of snow on the ground we were closed in for months.*

Harvey Gross and other South Lake Tahoe businessmen vigorously fought for clear roads, the key to winter business and successful ski areas. *Author's collection.*

> *So, to show it was possible, the residents of the South Shore hauled out their shovels, trekked up to Echo Summit and dug out the road themselves, calling the governor every other day to let him know how they were doing. It was sort of a party atmosphere, but serious business. We'd bring sandwiches and whiskey and start to work, sticking a bottle in the snow about 20 or 30 yards up the road and shoveling to it for refreshments. The crew managed about four miles every three days, then it would snow again and they would start over. But they proved it could be done, and Tahoe was on its way.*[89]

The California Highway Department began to make major improvements to Highway 50 in summer 1940. This was probably motivated more by the looming war and the necessity for transportation of goods and men rather than winter recreation. But it would prove to help the winter sports effort too. Grading started two miles east of Phillips and stretched three miles west of Meyers. A number of steep switchbacks were eliminated, and a 113-foot bridge was constructed.

Pressure from resort owners and the general public finally had an effect. On January 30, 1941, a resolution was passed urging the governor and the California Highway Commission to open Highway 50 immediately and keep it open every winter.

The road was kept open for the first time during the winter of 1941–42, but the government soon decided to conserve resources and use the men and machines to keep only Highway 40 open. Thus, the effects that World War II would have on winter recreation throughout the state had begun.

Once the war was over, winter sports promptly resumed along Highway 50. Resort owners from Placerville to South Lake Tahoe were making plans for the 1945–46 season. Ski runs were being cleared, and a number of ski tows were being installed. Highway 50 was going to be kept open over Echo Summit throughout the winter so travelers could reach South Lake Tahoe, Carson City and Reno.

By the end of 1948, skiing had fully recovered from the effects of World War II. There were twenty rope tows operating on Highway 50 from Kyburz to White Hills and talk of more to come. And the Highway 50 Association, with Ben Tarnutzer as publicity manager, promoted the Highway 50 areas with print advertising, using catchy slogans like "Ski Highway 50 in 1950," radio promotions and snow and road condition reports, all creating a united effort to endorse Highway 50 ski areas and lodging. These areas included White Hills, Bijou Park Ski-Way, Celio's

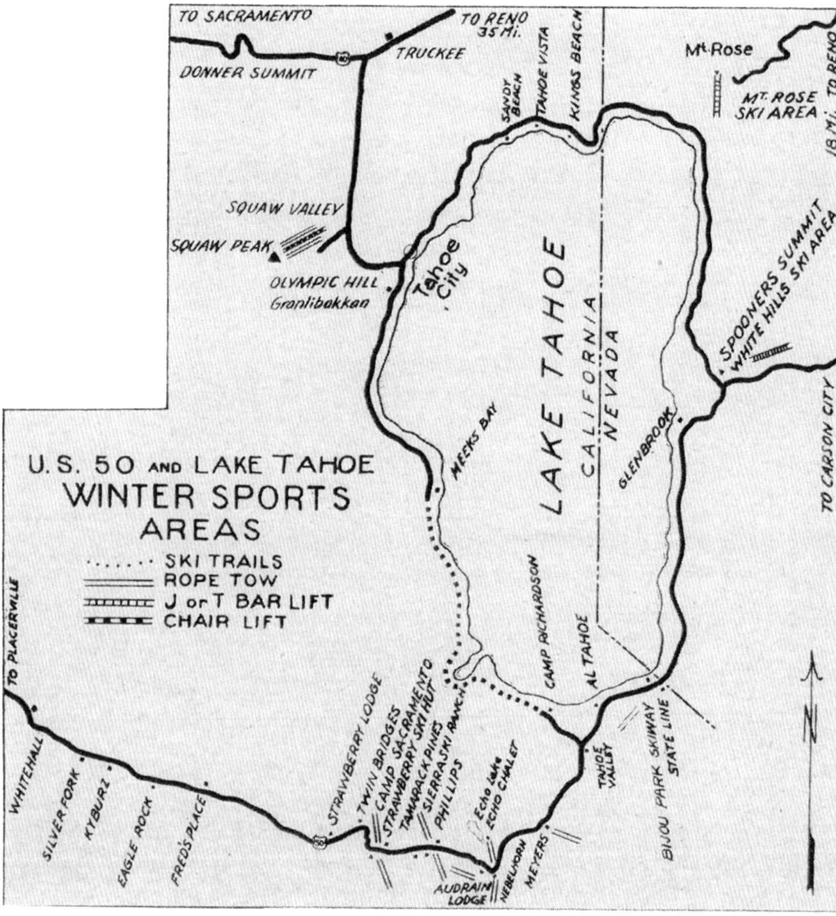

Map of ski areas along Highway 50, circa 1950. *Author's collection.*

Ski Ranch (sometimes also referred to as Celio's Triangle C), Flagpole Mountain, the Nebelhorn, Echo Chalet, Phillips, Sierra Ski Ranch, Strawberry Ski Hut and Strawberry Lodge. Of those areas, only Sierra Ski Ranch (now Sierra-at-Tahoe) exists today.

This chapter examines the origins of Highway 50's nine lost ski areas, the dedicated founders and owners of the areas, their effect on Lake Tahoe's skiing history and some of the factors that led to their demise.

STRAWBERRY LODGE

The Strawberry area has a long, vivid history, beginning as a Pony Express stop in the 1850s. According to former Strawberry Lodge owner Richard L. Mitchell, "The first, second, third, and fourth Strawberry Stations were all built within three-hundred yards of each other between 1858 and 1940."[90]

Located 179 miles east of San Francisco and 18 miles from Lake Tahoe, it is situated in the shadow of Pyramid Peak and next to a sheer granite monolith called Lover's Leap. It was a popular skiers' lodge in its heyday, and a December 1946 advertisement touted it as "a paradise of indoor comfort and outdoor sports, easily accessible by automobile or Greyhound as highway is greatly improved and kept open all Winter."

Fred Baumhoff, who had been successfully mining gold in Idaho in the 1930s, dreamed of developing a resort that would rival the recently opened Sun Valley. Baumhoff's childhood had been spent in Placerville, with frequent visits along the American River, so he decided this is where he would create his Sierra Sun Valley. In April 1939, he began negotiating with current owners, Mr. and Mrs. William Martin, to purchase the resort.

He modeled Strawberry Lodge after Sun Valley's Challenger Inn, Yosemite's Ahwahnee and Timberline Lodge at Mount Hood. He enlisted master stonemason Umberto Sabrialia to cut granite from nearby Lover's Leap to craft the stone walls and fireplaces. To attract visitors year-round, he provided horseback riding, a trout pond, a golf course, a bowling alley and skeet shooting.

The hotel opened on Memorial Day 1940. Baumhoff's dream came at a cost of $150,000. But America's entrance into World War II would prove to be ruinous to any chance of success for the lodge. His plan to build a ski lift up ten thousand foot Pyramid Peak came to a halt because steel supplies were limited to military use. And, as Mitchell wrote, "When Johnny marched off to war, nobody could, or would, come to Fred's lodge to play. Alpine skiing was now for fighting men schussing in Italian Alps."[91]

In December 1941, it was announced that Strawberry Lodge would remain open for the winter. The ski school was directed by Hans Sarbach, former director of the Timberline Lodge ski school. Baumhoff also built Strawberry Ski Hut in 1941 and outfitted it with a Constam T-bar in January 1942. The lift was "located in such a way as to provide the maximum variety of skiing opportunity for skiers in the various stages of experience, this new lift taps an area that will have an assortment of thrillways."[92] The T-bar was frequently

Left: Fred Baumhoff (*left*) built Strawberry Lodge in 1940 and Strawberry Ski Hut in 1941. *Courtesy of Idaho State Archives.*

Below: Fred Baumhoff modeled Strawberry Lodge after other renowned mountain lodges: Challenger Inn at Sun Valley, Yosemite's Awahnee and Timberline Lodge at Mount Hood. *Courtesy of Jimmy Petterson.*

featured in Strawberry Lodge brochures and advertisements even though it was located three miles east at Strawberry Ski Hut.

In 1943, Baumhoff sold Strawberry Lodge to Otto Schaefer, owner of Schaefer Meats in Oakland. The sale did not include Strawberry Ski Hut and its lift. Schaefer picked up where Baumhoff left off. He finished the tennis court, pool and golf course. With the addition of a curb around the tennis court, it doubled as a skating rink in the winter.

Advertisement for Strawberry Lodge and the T-bar at Strawberry Ski Hut. *Author's collection.*

Schaefer came to the United States from Germany when he was sixteen. He was already trained as a butcher and first landed in New Jersey. His sister encouraged him to go to California, where he started Schaefer Meats around 1941. Schaefer's Cold Storage continues to provide wholesale meat distribution today.

Once the war was over, with gas rationing and other travel restrictions coming to an end, life began to return to normal. By 1945–46, business had increased dramatically, so Schaefer hired Herb and Ollie Brook to manage the lodge. They brought skiing expertise to the operation, and skiers flocked to the nearby Strawberry Ski Hut T-bar, which whisked them 1,780 feet up the slope for twenty-five cents a ride.

Along with the new managers, many other improvements were added that season. Since Herb, a certified instructor, was busy managing the lodge, he hired Trodd Fortna to provide instruction. Fortna's ski school proved to be hugely popular, so Reserl Petterson filled in as his assistant on the busiest days. The large lodge was supplemented by a fourteen-unit

Left: Trodd Fortna managed the ski schools at Strawberry Lodge and Strawberry Ski Hut. *Author's collection.*

Right: Reserl Petterson, one of California's top woman ski instructors in the 1940s, provided ski instruction at Strawberry Lodge and Strawberry Ski Hut. *Author's collection.*

annex across the street, several cottages, a dining room, a coffee shop and a cocktail lounge.

In November 1948, Schaefer was granted a special-use permit to install a four-hundred-foot rope tow at Strawberry Lodge. A little beginners' hill was cleared at the annex across the highway from the main building. It was outfitted with a short rope tow, lights for night skiing and even a small jump. Guests now had their choice of using the rope tow at the lodge or traveling three miles to Strawberry Ski Hut to ride the T-bar.

Otto Schaefer's ownership ended in 1960, when he sold the lodge to Charlie Pavka. In the 1960s, South Lake Tahoe experienced a boom in development, and travel to the lake was seldom a problem in winter. But Strawberry Lodge suffered from increased competition from other Highway 50 areas.

The rope tow was removed in 1965. The Forest Service explained, "The tow was never a real money maker and was operated primarily for the convenience of guests. The hill had limited opportunity for the modern skier and with two full scale ski areas within a short drive, it seems unwarranted to activate the permit."[93]

Strawberry Lodge installed its first ski tow in late 1948. It was situated next to the annex across the street from the lodge. *Author's collection.*

Strawberry Lodge, circa 2018. Skiers can still stay in the historic lodge and find lift-served skiing eight miles up the road at Sierra-at-Tahoe. *Author's collection.*

After 1960, when Schaefer sold the lodge to Pavka, the business changed ownership a number of times, at one point being closed and boarded up. Ken and Bonnie Madsen purchased it in 1980, followed by Richard L. Mitchell and Bill Kier in 1983. By this time, the lodge was in dire need of repair and upgrading.

As Kier explained, "The lodge has been part of the history of the Sierra since the miners first opened a path to the gold and silver fields and called it Bonanza Road. In those days, of course, Bonanza Road was pretty rough and the lodge was a welcome sight to the miners. One writer described the road after a rainstorm as being '130 miles long and 5 feet deep.'"[94]

In its heyday, Strawberry Lodge provided much-needed lodging to Highway 50 skiers, and its little rope tow served skiers for seventeen years. The lodge is still operating today, but its days as a ski area are long over. It provides lodging, a bar and a restaurant for those visiting the beautiful surroundings along the American River. Strawberry Lodge and the

The Strawberry Lodge annex, circa 2018. It provided much-needed additional lodging on busy winter weekends, and skiers had rope tow access right outside their door. *Author's collection.*

shuttered annex are silent witnesses to the days of their former glory when skiers would flock to nearby slopes to ride the T-bar and stay in what was Baumhoff's Sierra Sun Valley.

STRAWBERRY SKI HUT–THE EDELWEISS

Strawberry Ski Hut was located 176 miles east of San Francisco and 15 miles west of Lake Tahoe. Fred Baumhoff, who had purchased Strawberry Lodge in 1939, built Strawberry Ski Hut in 1941 and installed the Constam T-bar in 1942, but with the advent of World War II, its use was limited until after the war. When he sold Strawberry Lodge in 1943, he retained ownership of Strawberry Ski Hut and its lift. But the end of World War II signaled the end of Baumhoff's ownership.

After the war, Charley McGuire and Mel Gautier owned and operated the area. They resumed operation of the 1,800-foot T-bar and opened the 1945–

Above: Charley McGuire (*left*) and Mel Gautier assumed ownership of Strawberry Ski Hut in 1945 and began operating the T-bar that had been installed before the war. *Author's collection.*

Opposite, top: Skiing boomed in the late 1940s and Strawberry Ski Hut was one of the most popular areas along Highway 50. *Courtesy of Jimmy Petterson.*

Opposite, bottom: Advertisement touting the many amenities for skiers at Strawberry Lodge and Strawberry Ski Hut. McGuire and Gautier renamed the hut Mt. Ralston Lodge, a name that would last for only a couple of seasons. *Author's collection.*

46 season with dormitory lodging for forty-five and a large cafeteria and après ski bar. McGuire and Gautier made extensive plans for the next season. They planned to invest $10,000 the following summer to add accommodations for an additional sixty skiers and build a new rope tow to complement the T-bar, adding an additional two thousand feet in length. The final touch would be

STRAWBERRY LODGE

On U. S. HIGHWAY 50

Between PLACERVILLE and Lake Tahoe

A paradise of indoor comfort and outdoor sports, easily accessible by automobile or Greyhound as highway is greatly improved and kept open all Winter. Distance from San Francisco and Bay Area only 185 miles.

SKI, SKATE OR RELAX

Fine Cuisine, Cocktail Lounge, Nightly Fun and Dancing with Emphasis on American Squares and International Folk Dances. Lighted Ice Skating Rink. Sport Shop and Rentals.

Write for Reservations to:
HERB AND OLLIE BROOK, STRAWBERRY LODGE, P. O. KYBURZ, CALIF.
For phone or wires specify: STRAWBERRY LODGE via TRUCKEE, CALIF.

MT. RALSTON LODGE (formerly Strawberry Ski Hut) and SKI LIFT . . .
Three Miles from Lodge

Modern T-Bar Constam Ski Lift 1,800 feet long with 420-foot rise . . . 25c per ride. Monday—Friday, $2.50 per day. New Rope Tow. Ski School Daily. Cafeteria and All Ski Services. Dormitory Accomodations.

Lift and Ski Hut owned and operated by:
CHARLES McGUIRE and MELVIN GAUTIER, P. O. KYBURZ, CALIF.
or Phone OAKLAND—GLencourt 8235

LARGE CLEARED PARKING AREA AT LODGE AND LIFT

Bill and Reserl Petterson were involved in the ownership, management and ski school at Strawberry Ski Hut. *Courtesy of Jimmy Petterson.*

clearing the slopes of rock and brush. Their efforts were supported by El Dorado National Forest officials who made every effort to keep the highway in good condition and provide plenty of parking for the crowds of skiers who flocked to the area on weekends.

In 1946, McGuire and Gautier renamed the ski hut Mt. Ralston Lodge after nearby Mount Ralston. Trodd Fortna was head of the ski school and was assisted by Reserl Petterson, both of whom were also teaching at Strawberry Lodge. Petterson would later have the distinction of being California's only certified woman ski instructor. The November 1, 1948 issue of *The Skier* reported that she was one of the few to pass the ski instructor's test held at Mammoth Mountain in April.

Herb Brook, former manager of Strawberry Lodge, San Francisco architect Norman Blanchard and Bill and Reserl Petterson purchased the hut and the skiing facilities in the summer of 1947. They changed the name back to Strawberry Ski Hut and immediately got to work and moved the rope tow and T-bar to the opposite side of the highway. The lift now operated on north-facing slopes, where skiing could last until May. During the winter of 1946–47, south-facing slopes were bare, while north-facing slopes were blanketed in snow. So, Brook knew that moving the

Brochure advertising the new lift, featuring the alluring ski slopes across the street from the hut. *Author's collection.*

tow to the north-facing slopes was key to maximizing skier days. He wrote, "A rope tow about 600' long will take skiers from the floor of the canyon, altitude 6,525', to a bench in the terrain, altitude 6,825'. At this point we will have the terminal of the Constam lift which is 1,800' long with a rise of 500'. The combined length therefore will be approximately 2,400' with a total rise of 700'."[95] The lift was powered by electricity with a gas engine available as a backup.

The Forest Service cleared over forty acres of timber on the north-facing slopes, "opening up a ski area of unsurpassed beauty and variety of terrain with runs for every type of skier."[96] A beginners' rope tow operated on a gentler slope, and the area was lighted for night skiing. Ever-important parking was available for about two hundred cars. There was excellent backcountry skiing and touring at nearby Ralston and Pyramid Peaks.

After all of the improvements were completed, the hut was as popular as ever. In an essay, writer Charles "Muddy" Watters showered the area with praise:

> *If ever Highway 50 has a professional ski hill to match the prowess of Sugar Bowl, Yosemite, Alta, and Sun Valley, then one must consider the plant developed at Strawberry Ski Hut. Represented here is an effort far exceeding anything attempted to date on the Placerville-Lake Tahoe route. A summertime of labor and ski engineering was expended to construct every possible trail and slope for the bunnies to the colorful expert.*[97]

The proliferation and popularity of the Highway 50 areas led to the formation of a new ski club, the Flying Fifty, in fall 1948. The Highway 50 Association formed the club along with the support of the resort operators in order to develop closer cooperation among the areas. Membership cards were five dollars and entitled members to discounts on ski tows and lodging. The

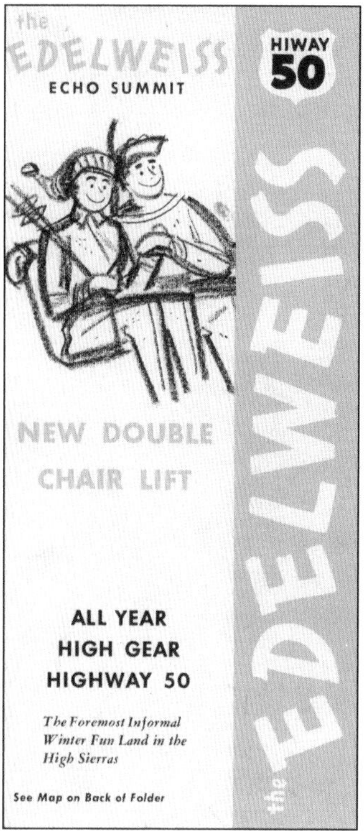

When Ken and Bunny Cotton purchased Strawberry Ski Hut, they renamed it the Edelweiss to better reflect the Bavarian-style changes they made to the building. *Courtesy of Lake Tahoe Historical Society.*

new club was also affiliated with the Far West Ski Association, enabling sanctioned meets at all of the Highway 50 tows. The inaugural directors of the club were Stub Hatch, Floyd Raffetto, Don Goodrich Jr., Kemp Moore and Joe Cola, with Herb Brook serving as secretary and racing chairman. Herb Poole, chairman of the Highway 50 association, predicted a membership of more than five hundred by year's end. The *California-Nevada Ski News* began promoting the new club in February 1949 with a special column titled "Winter Sports Flashes from Flying 50."

Not wasting any time, the club sponsored a major ski meet, the Pony Express Ski Races, at Strawberry Ski Hut on February 5–6, 1949. Men's and women's downhill and slalom events were held, with Warren Hart acting as course setter. The race drew skiers from all over the state, including University of California–Los Angeles, Yosemite Winter Club and the Reno Ski Club. That weekend, Highway 50 resorts were booked solid with skiers and visitors.

In late 1949, Ken Cotton, the former manager of the Johnsville Cotton Bowl, bought Herb Brook's interest in Strawberry Ski Hut. In fall 1950, Cotton and his wife, Bunny, redecorated the lodge with a Swiss mountain theme and renamed the lodge the Edelweiss to better reflect the look and décor. The Edelweiss became the new home of the Nebelhornets (now called the Redhornets), which had previously been at the Nebelhorn. An annex was added to increase accommodations. And, to enhance the Bavarian theme, the Edelweiss added a gift shop that featured cuckoo clocks, beer steins, Swiss houses and many other gifts imported from Switzerland and Germany. Aynedter took over ski instruction at Strawberry Lodge, the Edelweiss, and the Nebelhorn.

Lastly, improvements were made to the ski hill. A new rope was installed on the tow that fed the T-bar. Stumps and rocks were blasted from the hill, allowing earlier skiing on a better manicured slope. At this time, the Edelweiss and the Nebelhorn were the largest ski areas on Highway 50.

In 1953, Aynedter began making ambitious plans for an extensive new area at Lover's Leap, the massive monolith that looms high over Strawberry. He was motivated to develop the area because the terrain at Lover's Leap Ridge was unique in that all of its slopes, ridges, bowls and ravines were concentrated in one area and would offer the greatest variety of skiing for beginners to experts.

Aynedter described his bold plans, named "The Edelweiss Project Ski Area, Lover's Leap Ridge," for the press:

> *A modern, American-designed double chair lift, located in the center of the ski area, will take 600 skiers per hour to a point atop the ridge, 1800 feet above the valley floor. The length of the liftline will be more than 6000 feet. Two loading-unloading stations at approximately the first and second-third of the overall distance are designed to add to the variety of runs and to use the lift to its fullest capacity. Nine major courses, varying in length between 1¼ and 3½ miles, all starting from the same point at the top terminal of the lift, covering the eastern, northern and western exposure of the mountain, take the skiers down to the bottom terminal. The courses parallel to the liftline are breathtakingly steep in the upper sections and offer themselves as the ideal training ground for most advanced skiing. The more the runs deviate from the direct fall line the more gradual and gentle they become. The most outstanding of the intermediate runs is the one along the West Ridge which drops 2500 feet down, over a distance of 3¼ miles, past the majestic rock bluff of Lover's Leap, to Strawberry Lodge. A shuttle-bus service will take skiers back up to the bottom terminal at the Edelweiss.*[98]

One of the promotional efforts to raise money for the chairlift was a small publication titled "You Are Invited to Participate in a Chair Lift for the Edelweiss." "The Edelweiss Project," as the group called itself, was attempting to raise $175,000 to build the chairlift, enlarge the parking lot, construct a new lodge and remodel the current one. Plans also included a new warming hut and restaurant at the top of the ski run (8,300 feet) that would also serve as the upper terminal building. One of the main selling points was the easy accessibility to the lift:

> *Perhaps the outstanding attribute of this Sierra winter sports resort is accessibility. The resort buildings are 200 feet from the shoulder of all-year U.S. Highway 50. Parking facilities are immediately adjacent to the highway. The loading station for the ski lift is to be located less than 300*

Left: Lutz Aynedter hoped to install the first chairlift at the Edelweiss. He created this booklet to raise funds from investors. *Courtesy of Donner Summit Historical Society, Norm Sayler Collection.*

Right: A 1954 advertisement for the Edelweiss's first chairlift and the first on Highway 50. *Author's collection.*

> *feet from the highway and parking area. The great advantage to the skier of driving over a modern, fast highway to a large parking area, slipping into his skis and going a few yards to the loading station are evident. No other winter sports area in this part of the country can match this feature.*[99]

Aynedter's ambitious dream was never realized, but the Edelweiss did install the first chairlift on Highway 50 in fall 1954. In order to finance the lift, Cotton formed a corporation, inviting outside investors to purchase stock in the area. The stockholders were David Anderson, Walbam Inc., Richard C. Thompson, M.R. Gibbon Jr., Edward E. Hause, Melvin Black, Otto J. Bauer and Ellsworth LaBoyteaux. The Forest Service agreed that there was a public need for a chairlift at the Edelweiss and issued a permit in May 1953. Construction started in fall 1953, but the project was held up when early storms delayed progress.

The new Heron chairlift replaced the Constam T-bar. Its seventy-eight double chairs carried six hundred skiers per hour three-quarters of a mile up

Lover's Leap Ridge to an elevation of 7,250 feet, providing skiers with 750 feet of vertical. It began operating during the 1954 Christmas holiday, servicing runs up to three and a half miles in length. There was an intermediate loading station halfway up the slope, giving access to several trails adjacent to the main run. A beginners' rope tow was also in operation. Along with the new lift, owner Ken Cotton enlarged the parking lot and improved the lodge and ski shop.

In the first ten years under Cotton's ownership, the area grew from one building and six employees to three buildings and twenty employees, and it boasted the only double chairlift on Highway 50.

In its heyday, Strawberry Ski Hut was one of the most popular areas on Highway 50. It had one of the most active and successful junior ski clubs in California, the Redhornets, and developed successful racers such as Spider Sabich and Starr Walton. Much of the success of the club was due to the leadership of Lutz Aynedter.

In spite of its popularity and many improvements, the area was not without its problems. In 1961, Cotton left for Colorado, and Randall J. Schachtili managed the hut during the 1961–62 season. It was discovered that Cotton left more than $30,000 in unpaid bills. The Edelweiss Corporation was declared insolvent and ceased operations on May 31, 1962. The Forest Service canceled the permit to operate the Edelweiss Ski Area on November 1, 1962.

In early 1963, the Forest Service was exploring four different options to deal with the area:

1. Abandon the present use of the entire site completely and plant with trees. Complete site recovery.
2. Retain the present lodge and offer as a summer motel with swimming (a pool) and other summer attractions. Present indications are that the relocation of Highway 50 will not disturb this area. Eliminate the ski area with plans for complete site recovery.
3. Retain the present lodge as a part of the ski area for lodging purposes only. Continue the ski area but only under new development plans which places the lifts, new ski lodges, etc. south of the new Highway 50 above Camp Sacramento. Under this plan the present lodge could have no connection with the ski area development except to furnish needed lodging. It could be an annex to the operation or under separate management.
4. Some interest has been expressed for using the present lodges as an organization site.[100]

One last attempt was made to revive the Edelweiss in fall 1963. A group of ski enthusiasts led by Bill Young attempted to secure the Edelweiss permit, but the Forest Service declined to issue it. The Forest Service gave the following reasons for not issuing a new permit:

1. The elevation of the site is too low for reliable snow. This was one of the factors contributing to the bankruptcy.
2. A major scheduled relocation of U.S. Highway 50 will bisect the main ski slope in a few years.
3. Approved expansions of three existing ski areas located at higher elevations on U.S. Highway 50 (Sierra Ski Ranch, Echo Summit and Heavenly Valley) will adequately service the public winter sports needs in that portion of the El Dorado National Forest for several years ahead.[101]

The chairlift was removed in summer 1964. All that was left of the old ski operation were the remains of an old snow vehicle (Weasel), cargo sled, storage shed, lower terminal of the chairlift, scrap lumber from the T-bar terminals and debris from the snack bar. The Edelweiss and other buildings remained standing since they had previously been purchased by Otto Schaefer, owner of Strawberry Lodge. In October 1964, Assistant Regional Forester W.S. "Slim" Davis wrote,

> *The situation with the Chalets is that they now belong to Mr. Schaefer, who has been authorized by the court to remove them. He is now in Germany and will be away for a month or so. If they are not removed with what you consider a reasonable period, you should inform him the buildings are in trespass and ask of a removal commitment. If they are still there by early next summer, we should declare them abandoned in place and have a wrecker remove for salvage.*[102]

Two primary factors influenced the demise of the Edelweiss. The state was making plans to realign Highway 50, which would have affected the resort, but that project was never realized. And, like many other California lost ski areas, snow was unreliable at the Edelweiss, elevation 6,500 feet. Even so, under the direction of Herb Brook, Ken Cotton, Lutz Aynedter and Bill and Reserl Petterson, Strawberry Ski Hut thrived and was one of Highway 50's most popular areas in the 1940s and 1950s. It was home to Highway 50's first chairlift and was the training ground for hundreds of junior skiers and champion ski racers Spider Sabich, Ni Orsi and Starr Walton. In its heyday, the Edelweiss set the standard for ski areas along Highway 50 by developing clear, open slopes, installing a chairlift and providing instruction from some of California's best ski instructors.

Phillips

Phillips was first settled by the Phillips family in 1862 and was one of the many stage stops and waystations along historic Highway 50. It is located along the South Fork of the American River, two and a half miles west of Echo Summit.

Skiing history at Phillips started long before the first tows appeared. Joseph Wells Davis Phillips, the town's namesake, became acquainted with Snowshoe Thompson. Phillips's granddaughter Alice Lyon recalled that Snowshoe Thompson "stayed over nights on his return trips of Genoa and taught my grandfather to ski, using the long pole as a stabilizer and brake. He was one of our closest friends. There was a big pine that was struck by lightning and he used it to make skis. We called it the Snowshoe Thompson tree in his honor."[103]

Over the years, there were a number of different tow operators at Phillips. The first tow began operating during the 1941–42 season. It is unknown who installed and owned this tow, but the *Skier's Guide 1947* reported that Lyon and Sickles were running two rope tows, one six hundred feet, the other nine hundred feet, during the 1946–47 season.[104] So perhaps Lyon and Sickles ran the 1941–42 tow and resumed its operation once the war was over.

Additional ski tows sprang up at Phillips during the 1946–47 season. Howard Barnes operated one rope tow, which he dubbed Sierra Meadows, but Barnes's ownership was short-lived. During the 1947–48 season, he sold his Sierra Meadows ski tow to Francis Hodgkins, owner of the Phillips store. He also operated a small rope tow on the north side of Highway 50. Hodgkins's two rope tows continued to operate through 1960.

Another tow was owned by Ray and Floyd Barrett. The Barretts' operation started with one rope tow and a makeshift coffee shop. Parking was on the shoulder of Highway 50. Eventually, Ray became the sole owner and operator. He owned the area until early winter 1953, when he sold the area to Clinton Pratt. By this time, there were three rope tows and a 150-square-foot warming hut. Barrett's modest single rope tow operation eventually evolved into Sierra Ski Ranch, now Sierra-at-Tahoe.

A 1949 advertisement for Francis Hodgkins's resort at Phillips. *Author's collection.*

In the early 1960s, Phillips Pow-Wow Lodge began operating one rope tow and a toboggan tow. They eventually installed a second tow and continued to operate the lifts into the mid-1960s.

In its heyday, Phillips was a popular resort with cabins, a post office, store and Pow-Wow Lodge. Today, the property is still dotted with private cabins, but the lodge and other businesses have been gone for years. Phillips's only thriving business is Sierra-at-Tahoe Ski Area, the lone surviving ski resort on Highway 50 between Sacramento and Heavenly Valley.

ECHO CHALET

Echo Chalet, situated at 7,632 feet elevation on Highway 50, is in an idyllic location that provides stunning views of Echo Lakes and the surrounding mountains. Ski columnist Oliver Kerhlein described the unspoiled ski terrain at Echo Lakes: "There are excellent slopes facing both north and south at Echo Chalet with a rope tow in operation. Then, a short distance from the Chalet, nestling under Ralston Peak, there are any number of fine amphitheaters with slopes available for thousands of skiers."[105]

Echo Lake resort was built by Curt Rocca and opened for business on December 27, 1938. Rocca, a University of California–Berkeley graduate with a degree in forestry, wanted to leave the city life and responded to a Forest Service posting seeking a concessionaire to build a resort on Echo Lake.

The chalet was immediately popular, and all of the rooms quickly filled for New Year's Eve. The initial investment of $25,000 (borrowed from Rocca's father) covered the construction of a hotel with dormitory lodging for thirty people, a gas station, a boat house, a post office, a garage and a store. The chalet was open year-round, and a rope tow was operating by 1941.

In the beginning, only advanced skiers could access the skiing around Echo Lake. Rocca noted, "Until Highway 50 is kept open all winter, we will have to appeal to the experienced skier. I believe that when this takes place, Echo Lake and the surrounding country will be one of the most popular ski centers in the Sierras."[106] He also commented on the plentiful snowfall, an advantage he had over other areas at lower elevations on Highway 50: "At present we have more snow than any of the California skiing resorts. Seventy-five inches are on the ground at the present time, with snow still falling. In fact since the snow started we have had more fall here than in other ski centers. Our ski slopes are on the north side, therefore allowing little thaw."[107]

Rocca managed the chalet for the first year but was called to active duty in the navy in July 1940. Curt's mother, Blanche, thinking he would be gone for only a year, took over the management of the resort. She was at the helm of the chalet for the next five years.

In March 1941, resort and cabin owners were overjoyed when two rotary snowplows, one traveling from the Tahoe side and one traveling from Twin Bridges, opened the highway to vehicle traffic. There was still fifty inches of snow at Camp Sacramento and eighty-five inches of snow at Echo Summit, so spring skiing was expected to last into April. The first weekend the road was open, there were more than five hundred cars parked between Twin Bridges and Echo Summit, a distance of nine miles.

Residents and resort owners created a festive atmosphere that weekend, and the *Oakland Tribune* reported:

> *They are going to do their best to give everyone that comes up a swell time. Center of the celebration will be at Echo Chalet, where Kirk* [sic] *Rocca is planning ski races and other forms of amusement for skiers. Rocca's rope tow, 700 feet long, will operate all day Sunday free of charge and snowmobiles will run between the highway and the Chalet in order to furnish transportation to those who do not wish to ski over the one mile of snow-covered road.*[108]

The historic opening of Highway 50 that March created increased interest in Echo Summit as a prime ski area. Auburn Ski Club member and instructor Johnny Johansen constructed a rope tow near Echo Chalet in December

1941. His tow carried skiers from the highway to the crest above Echo Chalet. The tow was made up of two sections: one 1,200 feet long, the other 300 feet long, and was purported to be one of the longest in California.

The war years were challenging ones for the resort, as they were for most California ski centers. Curt's younger sister, Loellen Rocca Bonser, recalled the challenges they faced during those years: "We didn't know we were going to war. We thought he would have a year of service and come home. Mother was there to keep it running so we didn't lose our investment. It was very hard during the war to keep that place going."[109]

Blanche put in sixteen-hour days to make ends meet. During those war years, men were hard to come by, so she hired high school boys and girls to run the boat taxi and work in the store. Sometimes drifters who wandered in were put to work to repair motors and cook for guests. All of this was undertaken without electricity, which was not available during the war. Gas and rubber rationing was in full enforcement, reducing the number of vacationers coming to the lakes by car as well as limiting the fuel available for the boat taxis.

The Roccas sold the chalet after World War II, and it has since been owned by several other families. One family, the Jorgensens, operated Echo Chalet for more than twenty-five years, from 1946 until 1972.

Haven Jorgensen, who purchased the chalet from the Roccas, operated rope tows between 1946 and 1952. Jorgensen was a Sierra Club member and began going to Clair Tappaan Lodge in the early 1940s. He was not able to join the military because of poor eyesight, so he spent five years during the war managing the Clair Tappaan Lodge. In January 1946, he heard about Echo Chalet being for sale and ventured up to the area with one of his ski buddies. He recounted,

> *We parked off the highway and started skiing in, and about halfway we saw the Chalet tractor, nose into a hole where it broke down in eight or ten feet of snow. We got to the Chalet and it was all dark; I couldn't see the boathouse, what was there or anything. So my friend and I put our skis back on and skied across Lower Echo, to the top of Haypress Meadow, and there it was, Desolation all laid out before us. And I told my friend, I don't care what's back there, I can fix all of that. But* this *is what I've been looking for.*[110]

When first surveying the area, he explained, "The building was closed and looked foreboding. It was half buried in snow. There wasn't much to see. Desolation Valley looked so beautiful. I knew we could make a resort out of it."[111]

The rope tow didn't operate during the war but resumed operation in 1946. Guests wanting to leave the confines of the rope tow were transported by boat for access to Mount Ralston. At Ralston, adventurous skiers could ski a huge bowl with two thousand feet of vertical rise. A second tow was installed for the 1947–48 season, and the chalet offered ski lessons and ski tours of Mount Ralston. Ken Floto began managing the operation during the 1948–49 season. He had just returned from Germany, where he had served as an army officer.

The chalet was not accessible by car in winter, so skiers had to park on Highway 50. They could then ski the one mile into the resort or catch a ride on the resort's Weasel or Tucker Sno-Cat. There was a little telephone house by the side of the road where guests could summon a ride.

By early 1949, Echo Chalet had expanded and was operating three rope tows and offering ski touring into the backcountry of Mount Ralston, Desolation and the Crystal Range.

Jorgensen's ski operation ceased after the legendary winter of 1952. The Tahoe and Donner area experienced epic snowfall in January 1952, stranding 226 passengers in a Southern Pacific train at Yuba Gap. Those same heavy snows ended Jorgensen's winter operations at the chalet. He described the challenges encountered that winter:

> *1952 was one hell of a winter. Echo had 35 feet of pack. I kept putting tubes together and more tubes together, I thought I would never reach the bottom when I was measuring the snow pack. Many problems developed that season. I fell about 20 feet off the transformer room and hurt my back. I spent much of the winter in the hospital, plus I lost lots of equipment that year; so the family and I talked it over and decided that we could make it on the summer business, which was really increasing.*[112]

In the 1980s, a corporation briefly owned the resort as a tax write-off but allowed the building and other facilities to fall into disrepair. Tom and Kathleen "Kat" Fashinell bought the chalet from the corporation in 1984 and continue as owners today. Tom worked at the resort as a teenager when Jorgensen owned it. When they purchased it, they had no idea what running the resort would entail, but it has been a labor of love. They made improvements to the area and restored it to its former glory.

In 1993, with the backing of the Fashinells, the Rocca family placed a memorial to honor Blanche Rocca in the chalet parking lot. It is a fitting honor to the woman who guided Echo Chalet through what are likely its

Map of Echo Chalet featuring their ski tows and slopes. *Courtesy of Lake Tahoe Historical Society.*

Left: Before the war, skiers had to ski one mile to reach the chalet. After the war, a Tucker Sno-Cat and Weasel transported skiers from the road to the chalet. *Author's collection.*

Below: Skiers staying at the chalet had access to superb backcountry skiing near Mount Ralston. *Author's collection.*

A ski trek to Mount Ralston affords skiers a spectacular view of the Crystal Range, a group of spectacular mountain peaks in the Desolation Wilderness. *Author's collection.*

The chalet, circa 2018. Its days as a ski resort are long past, but it remains a popular summer resort. *Author's collection.*

most difficult and challenging years. Her memory lives on in the ongoing survival of the resort.

Even with all of the ownership changes over the years, the resort has retained its rustic charm and character. A visit to Echo Chalet today is like taking a step back in time. Kat Fashinell summed it up well:

> *It's family-run, friendly, and it's beautiful. I tell people it's like dropping back into the 50s. There are no TVs or radios. You hike, you fish, you read, you play games. Families hang out together and like it. Grandmas and Grandpas and kids play cards, they fish and tell stories, they get out their guitars and their kazoos and gut buckets. It is still like going to a funky Girl Scout camp or whatever. It really is.*[113]

THE NEBELHORN–ECHO SUMMIT SKI AREA

While serving in Europe in World War II, Gordon Stangland and Victor West operated the Nebelhorn cable car at Oberstdorf near the German-Austrian border. That experience inspired them to open a ski resort once they returned home. While in Germany, they met ex-German mountain trooper Lutz Aynedter, so the pair hoped to enlist him as their ski instructor once they opened their area. The *San Francisco Call Bulletin* reported that's exactly what happened:

> *Following their discharge from the Army, the two looked for a year in the Sierra mountains trying to find a location which appealed to them. Three years ago, they found that spot in a place at the crest of Highway 50 which they decided to call the Nebelhorn. Operating on a shoe string and buying their supplies from Army surplus, the two ex-soldiers obtained a 99-year lease on their present site and went to work. They cleared the mountainside, built a warming shack and two rope tows. Meantime, they had arranged for the entry into this country of Aynedter.*[114]

Stangland and West chose an area on Echo Summit with a base elevation of 7,350 feet. They began clearing slopes in the summer of 1947 and continued to prepare the area for the upcoming season. The area opened for business in early 1948.

Before lift-served areas were developed, adventurous skiers were attracted to the deep snows at Echo Summit, the highest point on Highway 50. *Author's collection.*

Gordon Stangland (*left*) and Victor West began work on the Nebelhorn during summer 1947. The area opened in early 1948. *Courtesy of Karen Stangland.*

During a tour of Tahoe areas in 1950, a newspaper reporter gave his impression of the facilities and slopes at the Nebelhorn:

> *This is the third season that genial Gordon Stangland has operated the Nebelhorn resort. There are no overnight accommodations. Just a warming hut with enormous fireplace including a snack-bar, and two husky rope tows leading to some of the finest ski slopes in the area. The thing that impressed me was the permanence and ruggedness of the facilities. The slopes are "fast" and I witnessed some of the most expert skiing the entire trip here. Although areas are set aside for beginners, I consider The Nebelhorn a place for the more advanced skiers to enjoy their sport.*[115]

Stangland, West and Aynedter formed the Nebelhorn Ski Club in February 1950. The club grew rapidly, and just days after it was formed, they had eighteen members, aged six to fourteen years. The club achieved as much or more notoriety than the ski area it was named for. While racing at Sugar Bowl in spring 1950, with their red hats and jackets, a nearby racer called them the Nebelhornets and the name stuck. In the 1950s, it was likely one of the most popular and active junior clubs in the state.

Much of the club's success can be attributed to Aynedter, who instituted a serious training program. All children who were aspiring racers were invited to join the club regardless of age or skill. The juniors progressed rapidly and began to demonstrate real ability under Aynedter's leadership.

Aynedter taught the young skiers a "power skiing" technique that he adopted from his instructor, Austria's great Toni Seelos. "They instruct the use of momentum and shifting of body weight to accomplish smoothly the high-speed maneuvering once accomplished by great exertion and near-defiance of the laws of motion and centrifugal force. It works best, Aynedter says, when it is learned at an early age and before other bad habits are acquired."[116]

Aynedter later reminisced about the early days of the club:

> *In this area, where skiing still was new, and undeveloped, a group of parents were, not only encouraging its bevy of offspring in the gentle art of the boards, but was attempting, also, to bring about some kind of organization, in the interest of uniform effort, and increased efficiency. And, soon, the imminence of talent was not to be denied. Interest among parents was increasingly stimulated, and joined in. In those days, it was the Nebelhorn Ski Area that generously placed all its facilities at our disposal. We did not ski against the clock, and we did not ski for laurels. We skied because it was fun, because it*

Above: The original Nebelhorn lodge, winter 1947–48. *Courtesy of Karen Stangland.*

Right: Skiers ride one of the Nebelhorn's rope tows. *Courtesy of Karen Stangland.*

Under Aynedter's tutelage, the Nebelhornets developed outstanding racing technique. *Courtesy of Karen Stangland.*

> *was a thrill to cut trails through new powder snow, and breathe the beauty of the winter mountains. From this, the Nebelhorn Ski Club was born.*[117]

Race training for the club was initiated in the second season (1950–51). The kids were successful, winning medals and finishing well in races at Yosemite and Tahoe City. The 1951–52 season was marred by setbacks. Storms interrupted regular training, discouraged parents removed their children from participation and a new training ground had to be found.

The club weathered the challenges of that season and survived, team spirit and solidarity winning out. As Aynedter recounted, "The storms blew over, and we were again packing our slalom courses. This time it was the Edelweiss Ski Resort, with its rugged racing course, beautiful back trails, and cozy atmosphere, that offered shelter and facilities to the team."[118] Since the club was no longer affiliated with the Nebelhorn, Aynedter renamed them the Redhornets.

Aynedter came to the United States in 1949, though he had first applied for a visa in 1939 when Hitler invaded Czechoslovakia, where he was a bright young ski star. In 1937, he won the Czechoslovakian Junior Championship and

Lutz Aynedter influenced skiing throughout the Lake Tahoe area. He instructed at the Edelweiss, Strawberry Lodge and the Nebelhorn and had a hand in planning Heavenly Valley. *Courtesy of Karen Stangland.*

the German Junior Championship, a feat that he repeated in 1938. In 1939, he served as both coach and captain of the Charles University ski team in Prague. Forced to remain in Europe, he became an instructor for the mountain troops and served under Rommel in Africa. He directed sixteen instructors at the original Nebelhorn ski school in the Bavarian Alps.

Once he arrived in California, Aynedter made an impact all over the Tahoe area. After his stint at the Nebelhorn, he went on to the Edelweiss and made extensive plans to develop the area around Lover's Leap (see the Edelweiss section, page 85). He designed a ski jump at Bijou Park Ski-Way during the 1954–55 season. In the mid-1950s, he presented a thirteen-week dry ski school on television. The thirty-minute program aired every Thursday night on a Sacramento station and was sponsored by local ski shops. By December 1950, he was the ski school director at three Highway 50 areas: the Edelweiss, Strawberry Lodge and the Nebelhorn.

When construction began at Heavenly Valley in 1955, Aynedter was hired to create the preliminary planning for the area. In addition to being a skilled skier and instructor, he was also an architect.

In the early 1960s, after many years of experience as a ski instructor and ski area planner, Aynedter, in partnership with civil engineer J.P. Ramer, went into business as a ski consultant. They offered ski area development, ski jump and ice rink design, ground and snow profiles for lift lines, road layouts and other engineering services.

Stangland and West's ownership ended when Charles and Glatha Drace purchased the Nebelhorn in October 1951. The ski school remained under the direction of Aynedter and his assistant Godie Schuetz. The new owners focused on improving the hill and encouraging junior skiing. Drace created a new racecourse at the Nebelhorn, which was built to Class A specifications. His plan was for all of the slopes at the Nebelhorn to be comparable to major European ski slopes.

In 1951–52, they finalized a program to provide a winter physical education program for local elementary and high school students. Every first through twelfth grader was offered a ski lesson with an additional hour of supervised practice twice a week. Instruction ranged from beginning to advanced racing.

The Draces owned and operated the Nebelhorn for five seasons, selling it to Steve and Jean Myers in 1956. The Nebelhorn now had a new owner and a new name. The Myerses renamed the resort Echo Summit Ski Area, a name most skiers were already calling the area before the official name change. Myers improved the road into the parking area and purchased a snowplow to keep the road clear. He also remodeled the lodge and added a new ski shop and snack bar.

Three rope tows were operating at this time, so for the 1957–58 season, plans were made to double the length of the intermediate rope tow and to have a new T-bar in place by Christmas 1958. That much-anticipated T-bar began operating during the 1958–59 season and opened up 40 percent more terrain.

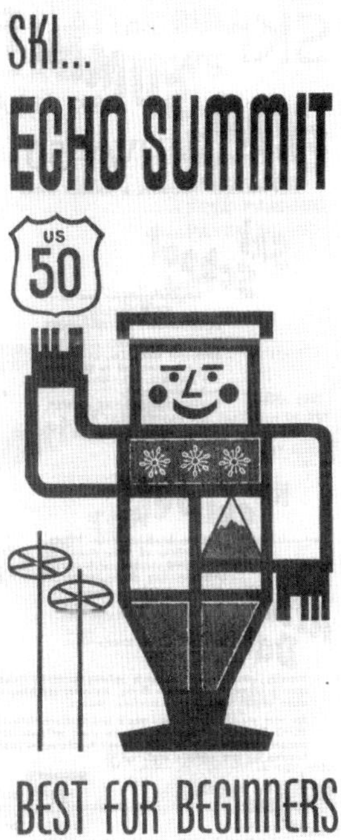

In 1956, Steve Myers took over ownership of the Nebelhorn and renamed it Echo Summit Ski Area. *Author's collection.*

By 1966, Echo Summit and other small areas were struggling to compete against the larger areas in the Tahoe basin, such as Heavenly Valley and Squaw Valley. Skiers were spending more money and expected chairlifts, gondolas, restaurants, bars and other amenities. Steve Myers commented, "Areas like mine just can't keep going without a good deal of added expense for expansion. Right now I am looking for someone to buy Echo."[119]

Bill Young bought the resort in 1972, and by 1973, he was operating three rope tows and a platter pull. But Young decided to close Echo Summit in 1974 because the facilities were old and potentially dangerous. Then, vandals burned down the lodge. He attempted to reopen it as Ski Echo Tahoe for the 1979–80 season. It was due to open with a day lodge built from four railroad cars and two double chairlifts serving eight runs. Apparently, Young was not able to make the needed upgrades to the area and was unable to open for the 1979–80 season. Echo Summit would once again have a new owner. Steve

Hayward, former general manager at June Mountain, bought the area in December 1980.

Hayward completed a number of improvements by the time the new Echo Summit opened for the 1981–82 season. A new 9,000-square-foot day lodge, designed by Reno's Peter Wilday, was completed. The building was furnished with a kitchen, dining area, restrooms, retail shop, offices and an upstairs loft. The kitchen could serve 500–600 people per day. The exterior was outfitted with a deck to provide seating for 150–200 skiers. And, most importantly, the area now had two chairlifts. They were partially installed when Hayward took over, and installation was finished under his watch. So, the long-planned chairlifts had finally become a reality. The parking lot had a capacity of about three hundred cars. The new owners hoped to expand and make additional improvements in the future, especially since the area had only six ski runs. They had received approval for a third chairlift and were making plans to develop the upper mountain. Echo Summit had 500 feet of vertical feet at this time. Opening the upper slopes would increase that to 1,200 feet. That development was key to opening up challenging terrain for all levels of skiers and could make or break the future of the area.

Sno-Tek O'Connor prepared an Echo Summit Ski Area Development Plan in 1985. Management knew that adding more acreage, especially more advanced runs, was critical to the viability of the area. The report noted that ski area use was low but increasing. There was no advanced skiing at the area, and the plan noted that it was remarkable that use was as high as it was without any advanced skiing. Other local areas experienced ten to twenty times more use and had higher lift ticket prices. Sno-Tek recommended the ski area expand to include more advanced terrain to the south. And the Forest Service noted that the vertical drop at Echo Summit is 500 feet, concluding, "Average skier needs are 20,000–25,000 vertical feet of skiing in a day. At the Echo Summit site this would equate to 40 trips up the ski lift. As skiers become more experienced, they move on to more challenging sites, making it difficult for Echo Summit to get repeat business."[120]

The area struggled through the 1980s, due to competition from larger areas and lack of snow during some drought years. A four-to-five-year drought plagued California ski areas in the late 1980s. Echo Summit Ski Area was known as a beginners' area with only five hundred feet of vertical drop. Skiers seeking more challenging terrain would go somewhere other than Echo Summit for longer and more advanced runs. All of these factors made it difficult for the area to remain a viable business, closing permanently in 1988. The Small Business Administration (SBA) bought the area in 1989. The

Forest Service then purchased the area from the SBA in 1990. At this time, there was a Sno-Park for winter parking and snow play at the area. The ski lodge had been boarded up, and the ski lifts stood idle. The historic area had become a ski area ghost town.

The Forest Service explained the difficulties that small ski areas faced in the 1980s and 1990s:

> *Looking beyond the recent drought conditions, annual growth rates in the downhill ski industry have been relatively flat. The average annual growth for the California and Nevada Region was 3.1 percent over the 5-year period 1986/87–1990/91. This is lower than the inflation rate of 4 percent for that period. It is difficult for beginner ski areas to survive on 3 percent growth. With costs increasing faster than demand, numerous small ski areas have gone out of business in recent years. Since the numbers of skiers have not gone up substantially, larger ski areas are retrofitting and adding amenities to increase their market share.*[121]

The Forest Service went to work to determine what direction to take with the area. In September 1992, it published *Draft Environmental Impact Statement on Future Use of the Echo Summit Ski Area Site*. Based on that report, it proposed a number of options for the future of the site. In 1993, the Forest Service wrote, "The USDA Forest Service proposes to issue a special use permit or Memorandum of Understanding (MOU) for operation and management of the former Echo Summit Ski Area lodge and to remove lifts and other facilities at the site which are not compatible with the selected use."[122]

The final impact statement also spelled out Forest Service concerns about the current state of the area:

> *The current condition of the former ski area facilities being vacant and unused is not consistent with* Eldorado National Forest Land and Resource Management Plan *direction. Although a portion of the site is being used for dispersed snow play in conjunction with the State operated Sno-Park, the lodge and other ski area facilities are not being used for public benefit. Since the site is no longer occupied or managed by a permittee, public safety, deferred maintenance, and the potential for vandalism are major concerns contributing to the need for this environmental impact statement.*[123]

These concerns prompted the Forest Service to remove the two chairlifts and rope tows in 1998.

The Echo Summit ski slopes that were first developed more than seventy years ago are still visible today. *Author's collection.*

The alpine-style day lodge was brought back to life by Adventure Mountain owners Jim and Linda Mueller. *Author's collection.*

The area continued to remain idle for a number of years and would never operate as a ski resort again. Jim and Linda Mueller purchased the property in 2006, making substantial improvements to open it as Adventure Mountain, a snow play area. Today they offer machine-groomed sledding, tubing and snow play. They have remodeled the lodge where visitors can warm up by a fire and have lunch at the Mountainside Café. So, the slopes of the historic Nebelhorn no longer serve skiers, but they do provide perfect terrain for other kinds of winter fun.

FLAGPOLE MOUNTAIN

Flagpole Mountain Ski Area was located at the foot of Meyers grade. Jack Hughes opened the area in 1948 with two rope tows, one 1,500 feet long with a 500-foot rise and the other 800 feet long with a 300-foot rise. He expected an influx of skiers for the opening and completed a clearing for a parking lot in November 1948.

After the 1948–49 season, plans were being made for the following winter. In spring 1949, manager Roy Wold offered Bay Area ski clubs a free parcel of land near the area to build their own ski lodge. And there were plans to build two more tows, but the area never opened during the 1949–50 season.

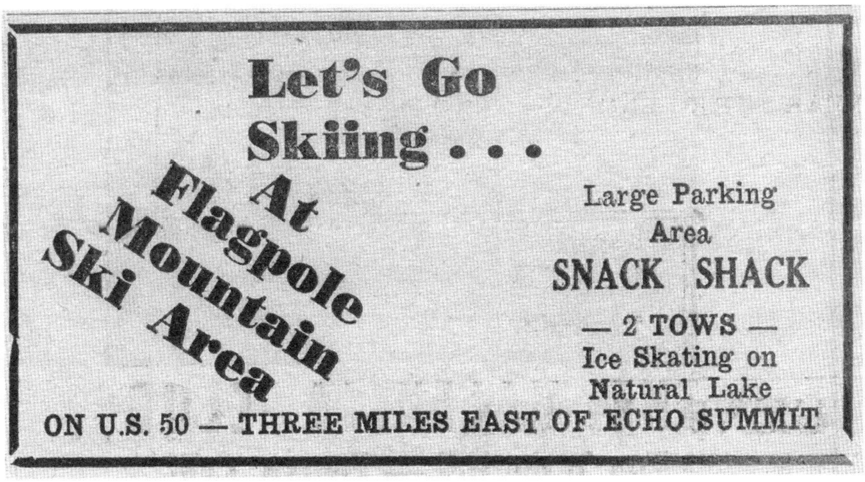

A January 1949 advertisement for Flagpole Mountain Ski Area. The area was only open for one season, 1948–49. *Author's collection.*

It is difficult to pinpoint where the slopes of the ski area once lay. Flagpole Mountain can be seen in the distance, towering above what would have been the location of Flagpole Mountain Ski Area. *Author's collection.*

It is unknown why Flagpole only survived one season. Nearby Strawberry Ski Hut and the Nebelhorn were larger and very popular, so it is possible Flagpole Mountain didn't have the necessary facilities and slopes to draw skiers to the area.

CELIO'S LAKE VALLEY SKI RANCH

The Celio family has a prolific history at Meyers. Formerly called Lake Valley, it was home to a Pony Express station (known as Yank's Express Station), hotel and stage stop between Carson City and Placerville. The area was eventually renamed for George Meyers, who purchased property in 1873. Meyers sold the town and 1,400 acres to Carlo G. Celio in 1903.

Carlo G. Celio and his family arrived in California in 1853 and eventually settled in Upper Lake Valley in 1863. By the late 1800s, the Celio businesses included dairy farming and cattle ranching. In 1905, the business incorporated as C.G. Celio & Sons Inc. and had become the largest employer at the south end of Lake Tahoe.

By the mid-1930s, Norm Celio, one of Carlo's grandsons, managed much of the family's holdings, including the lumber mill, a cattle ranch and the town of Meyers. He would be involved in the family business, including skiing, for more than fifty years. He was also involved in a number of community business associations. When the Lake Tahoe Service Club was founded in summer 1937, one of its main objectives was to improve highway conditions and winter business. Norm Celio was its first president.

Continuing to focus on an all-year highway in and around South Lake Tahoe, Celio became a director of the El Dorado branch of the chamber of commerce in 1939. It was reported that the group planned "a program of publicity and development for the year in which an important item will be to secure an all year open highway over Echo summit. During the past term this branch was instrumental in accomplishing snow removal through the winter season on roads of the south eastern lake shores and the Lake Valley district."[124]

When the Lake Tahoe Chamber of Commerce organized in December 1948, Celio became the director representing the Meyers area. In 1954, he became president of the organization, which was now known as the Lake Tahoe–Sierra Chamber of Commerce.

The area around Meyers doesn't look like promising ski terrain, but in 1946, Cortlandt Hill, along with Hannes Schneider and Luggi Foeger, conducted

Long before Norm Celio installed his ski tow, early residents at Meyers used skis for transportation and other activities. *Courtesy of Lake Tahoe Historical Society.*

A December 1947 advertisement for the Celio family ski area located at Meyers. *Author's collection.*

an aerial survey of the Cascades, Sierra Nevada and Southern California mountains, which they later followed up with an on-the-ground survey of possible locations for successful ski areas. They reported that Meyers had a "gradient suitable for intermediate and beginners. Good practice slope."[125]

C.G. Celio & Sons struggled through World War II to keep the family businesses afloat. After the war, with tourism and travel returning to normal, Norm and his brother-in-law decided to build a rope tow near their icehouse on what is now the Tahoe Paradise Golf Course. The 1,000-foot tow, with a 150-foot rise, began operating in December 1945. Improvements were made to the tow the following season, and Webb Terwiliger, a former recreation director in the navy, operated his ski school at Meyers during the 1945–46 season.

Celio called his ski tow Celio's Lake Valley Ski Ranch, but the California State Chamber of Commerce, in its yearly winter sports guide, just referred to the area as Meyers Station. It was also sometimes called Celio's Triangle C. The tow operated for six winters, its last being the 1950–51 season. In 1950, the Celios sold all of their holdings, marking the end of C.G. Celio & Sons. The town of Meyers, with its 1,600 acres and 22 buildings, was purchased by the Saugstad family. The Saugstads owned the Roseville Ford dealership where the Celios had purchased their vehicles. The end of C.G. Celio & Sons also marked the end of Celio's Lake Valley Ski Ranch.

Bijou Park Ski-Way

Plans for winter recreation facilities at the Bijou Park area near Stateline in South Lake Tahoe began in summer 1940. John Keller, who owned extensive property in the area, invested $10,000 to develop a ski run. The following summer, Keller was developing summer homes on 1,200 acres in the area, and the *Placerville Mountain Democrat* announced that "Bijou Park Boulevard is an excellent ski hill and winter ice skating is an attraction on a three-acre rink."[126]

In November 1941, Keller was making preparations to install an upski on his ski hill. It is unknown if the tow was ever built and, if so, how long it operated. Bijou Park would have to wait until after World War II for a new entrepreneur to operate a ski tow in the area.

Lee Miller installed a portable rope tow powered by a gas engine during the 1948–49 season. The new tow, dubbed Bijou Park Ski-Way, was located south

A January 1949 advertisement for Bijou Park Ski-Way. *Author's collection.*

of Pioneer Trail and Ski Run Boulevard. The modest slopes, outfitted with a small warming hut, provided adequate skiing for beginners and families and operated over the years with one to three rope tows. Shortly after it opened, Miller outfitted the one-thousand-foot ski run with lights.

Miller enlisted Owen Evans to serve as ski instructor, and in January 1949, they established a junior program. Sponsored by the Tahoe-Sierra Sportsman's Club and the Bijou Park Ski-Way, forty-nine children signed up for the program. Evans and Jack Hughes, owner of Flagpole Mountain Ski Area, assisted with the youngsters' two-hour lesson. Miller sold his little rope tow area to Bill Sutherland in 1951. He made a number of improvements to the area, adding electric power for the tow and a second rope tow, and built a permanent warming hut outfitted with ski rentals and snack bar. Sutherland then sold the area to its third owner, Chris Kuraisa, in 1954.

Kuraisa moved to Tahoe from Oakland in 1953 and soon after purchased a sporting goods store in South Lake Tahoe, not far from Stateline. At this time, few tourists visited in winter except for those frequenting the casinos or the few ski areas around the lake. Wanting to increase winter revenue, he bought six hundred pairs of ice skates at a closeout sale. He opened his own skating rink and, shortly thereafter, in February 1954, bought Bijou Park Ski-Way from Sutherland for $1,950. Kuraisa recalled that

> *Sutherland offered to sell me his two-rope tow area called the Bijou Ski Run for $1,950 and the property for $3,750. I felt the ski area would complement the sport shop. Besides I loved to ski. A lot of people thought I was crazy. Skiing wasn't that big. When I told my wife what I'd done, she started crying. She said, "You've spent all the eating money!"*[127]

Kuraisa was a hands-on owner, operating and maintaining the tows, selling tickets and managing the sporting goods store. And the little area was a money maker. During Kuraisa's first season at the helm, there was more than

Left: Chris Kuraisa operated Bijou Park Ski-Way for one season, then developed Heavenly Valley, whose inaugural season was 1955–56. *Author's collection.*

Below: *From left to right*: George Cannon, Philip "Curly" Musso, Rudy Gersick and Chris Kuraisa at the top of Heavenly's Gunbarrel chair. Ski writer Carson White called them "The big four of Heavenly Valley." *Author's collection.*

a $5,000 profit. And lift tickets were selling for only $1. During the second season, the rope tows were running on electric motors, and the area continued to be popular with skiers.

He also began to explore the surrounding mountains that towered over his area and began to dream of a much bigger resort. He secured some business partners and developed a master plan for a ski area stretching all the way to the top of Monument Peak.

Rudy and Trudy Gersick had also moved to South Lake Tahoe from Oakland and were the new owners of Ski Run Lodge. They soon met Kuraisa, and while visiting Bijou Park Ski-Way, Rudy commented to Kuraisa, "What a wonderful spot for a chairlift!" Kuraisa replied, "I've been thinking that for a long time."[128] The pair then teamed up with George Canon and Philip Musso, and the group raised enough capital to install a double chairlift, four rope tows and a warming hut at the top of the chairlift. That was the beginning of Heavenly Valley, what is now one of California's most popular resorts, but it spelled the end of the Bijou Park Ski-Way.

Heavenly Valley opened in December 1955, and once skiers started flocking to Heavenly, Kuraisa stopped operating his tows at Bijou. The area had operated for seven seasons and was one of South Lake Tahoe's pioneer ski areas. Heavenly Valley continues to dominate the alpine ski scene in South Lake Tahoe, and Bijou Park Ski-Way has long been forgotten. The old Bijou Park ski slopes are now dotted with homes. The mountains towering far above the pioneer ski area are now part of Heavenly Valley, home to some of California's and Nevada's favorite ski runs.

WHITE HILLS SKI AREA

White Hills Ski Area owner William Bliss and Warren Hart, manager, were guest speakers at an October 1946 Kiwanis meeting to announce the opening of their new ski resort. It was located on Highway 50 at Spooner Summit, twelve miles west of Carson City and forty-two miles from Reno. Work had begun in summer 1946, and the new area was ready to open for the 1946–47 season.

Hart, who had previously operated a tow at Mount Rose, became the first manager of the area. He had been a paratrooper with the Tenth Mountain Division in Italy and taught ski troops at Camp Hale, Colorado.

Before work began on White Hills, Spooner Summit had a jumping hill and cross-country ski course that was the location of the February 1946 California

William Bliss hired Warren Hart, shown here with Dodie Post, to be the manager of White Hills Ski Resort. *Author's collection.*

Ski Jumping Championships and the Snowshoe Thompson Memorial Cross-Country ski race. There was ample parking, and road crews worked to keep the highway free of snow, so it already had the makings of a ski resort.

In August 1946, Bliss signed the contract for construction of a Constam T-bar on his property, which was located almost directly across the highway from the previously constructed ski jump. He also stated that "if members of Douglas county and Carson City ski clubs desire a championship type of jump [it] also will be constructed in the area so that it may be utilized for future international events."[129]

Bliss believed that "Douglas county's year-around vacation area at Lake Tahoe, because of its ideal mountain terrain and close proximity to the densely populated areas of California is destined to become even better known as a winter resort than it now is as a summer resort."[130] And there were those who, encouraged by the development of White Hills, were "enthusiastic concerning the proposed improvements [and] are visioning a day when the Lake Tahoe area will surpass the widely advertised Idaho resort of Sun Valley for its winter sports opportunities."[131]

Once the materials for the T-bar arrived, Constam's Charles Van Evera and a crew of workers were ready to help construct the 2,200-foot lift. Snow was slow in coming, so work continued on the area through December. They were hoping to have the T-bar ready for opening day and were sculpting a ski jumping hill when the bulldozer became stuck. Hart summed up the challenges they faced: "It's real tough going," he said. "It took a crew of men and a tow truck, brought over from Donner Summit for the job, working all night during a snowstorm to extricate the heavy piece of equipment which is being used to complete the profile of the new jumping hill."[132]

Skiers flocked to the area when it finally opened. On December 29, 1946, there were three hundred skiers on the slopes, and they were only running a rope tow. That first season, White Hills hosted two major ski meets. The 1947 California State Jumping Championships took place there on February 1 and 2. This was also the preliminary tryout for California and Nevada jumpers hoping to compete at the 1948 Winter Olympic Games at St. Moritz. And White Hills continued to host the annual Snowshoe Thompson Cross-Country Memorial Race.

Surprisingly, the area seemed to be better known for jumping meets and the Snowshoe Thompson Memorial Race than for alpine skiing. The 1947 meet, featuring ski jumping and the historic Snowshoe Thompson race, saw ten thousand spectators, and the organizers of the 1948 meet expected even more.

Charles Van Evera oversaw the installation of the T-bar at White Hills. He was a ski lift expert, having planned and installed lifts at a number of other areas. *Author's collection.*

With all of the first-year glitches worked out, Hart was anxiously awaiting White Hills's second season. The T-bar was ready, and the troubles encountered the inaugural year had been remedied. During the first year, the crossbars were continually breaking and had to be replaced with new ones. The fallen trees and stumps that littered the face of the mountain had been removed and the slopes brushed out. The area now had six excellent runs from 2,200 feet to one and a half miles in length. In addition to the T-bar, two rope tows serviced beginner runs. A warming hut, coffee shop, bar and ski rental shop rounded out the facilities. The area would again play host to a number of special events, including the Snowshoe Thompson Memorial Race, Nevada State A, B, C, D jumping championships and many other local and White Hills Ski Club events. The White Hills Ski Club formed in fall 1948, replacing the recently dissolved Douglas County Ski Club.

The main slope at White Hills, served by the Constam T-bar. *Author's collection.*

The former White Hills Ski Area as it looks today. Trees have not yet fully obscured the ski run, still just visible in the center of the photograph. *Author's collection.*

Warren Hart managed White Hills for its first three seasons, selling his interest in the area in November 1949 to return full time to his Reno insurance business. White Hills Ski Area continued in business for six more seasons, closing permanently in 1955. Heavy snow brought throngs of skiers to White Hills in January 1955, but the 1954–55 season would be the last season the area operated. By this time, the area was only running a nine-hundred-foot-long rope tow, under the direction of Ernie Lee and Ken Amundson, and was open only on the weekends. Reno Ski Bowl opened in 1953, likely drawing Reno residents away from White Hills. And nearby Heavenly Valley, with its double chairlift and handful of rope tows, opened in December 1955, presenting another serious challenge to White Hills skier numbers. With other larger and better-equipped areas nearby, White Hills struggled to attract skiers to their lone rope tow, ending its nine seasons as a ski area.

6

HIGHWAY 40

Like U.S. Highway 50, U.S. Highway 40 (now Interstate 80), had its origins in the nineteenth century. In June 1864, Leland Stanford, Mark Hopkins, Collis P. Huntington and Charles Crocker opened the Dutch Flat and Donner Lake Wagon Road. During the gold rush, wagons and stagecoaches traveled along the route carrying passengers and supplies. But when the Central Pacific reached Colfax in September 1865, the railroad was the preferred and only mode of mechanized transportation in winter. It was this accessibility by rail that led to Truckee and other areas on Donner Summit to become California's first winter sports areas.

Norden, near the top of Donner Summit, was described as perfect for winter sports: "Accessible in winter by train, plentiful snowfall, long season, and open slopes."[133] By the end of the 1940–41 season, it was estimated that there were more ski lifts along Highway 40 than in any other winter sports area in the United States. Over $100,000 had been invested in ski tows, J-bars and chairlifts. The Tahoe National Forest office provided skiers with detailed information about the lifts:

> *Highway 40 area: At the Sugar Bowl there are two rope tows and the giant chairlift. At Soda Springs two rope tows and a J-bar are operated. At Donner summit, opposite Vanderford's, two rope tows are located. To the south of the summit maintenance station a long rope tow will be found by following the Sierra Crest ski trail to the edge of Lake Mary. At the S.P. Station at Norden a rope tow has been recently installed, mainly for the use of patrons*

> *of snow train specials but open to the public. The Sierra Club maintains a double tow about one-half mile north of U.S. 40 but club members usually tax this improvement to the limit. Below Soda Springs the next lift is found at Rainbow Tavern which is of the J-bar type and located directly back of the hotel. The Auburn Ski Club has moved its rope to a new location, still on the club grounds, but which affords a much better down-hill run this year. Cisco Grove has a new rope tow recently put in operation opposite the resort. At the forest service hill at Yuba Gap, four miles east of Emigrant Gap, a rope tow has been constructed this season. Pioneer Camp, one mile east of Emigrant Gap, runs a rope tow.*[134]

In the late 1930s, skiing was surging in popularity because of the proliferation of ski tows, but skiing came to a virtual standstill because of wartime restrictions and closures. But after the war, skiing crowds soon returned. Skiing along Highway 40 was in better shape than ever to accommodate the postwar skiing boom. There were new and improved lodging, more parking and first aid stations. Donner Summit Lodge had been expanded, and other lodges were anxious and ready for skiers to return.

By the end of the 1930s, Highway 40 had become a mecca for skiers. Ski areas lined the route from Laing's Pioneer Camp to Donner Summit. *Author's collection.*

By the late 1940s, skiing had fully recovered from the effects of the war. In 1947, David R. Brower, longtime Sierra Club member and director, wrote, "The most used ski area in the Sierra lies along Highway 40 and the Southern Pacific."[135] Another reporter acknowledged, "For the first time this season, automobiles carrying skis on their racks on Highway 40 outnumbered ordinary travelers."[136] And the *Donner Trail Reporter* wrote that there were twenty lodges between Emigrant Gap and the Nevada state line that were open year-round. They also reported that there were over twenty thousand feet of ski tows in operation along the Donner Trail.

Ski business owners and operators decided to make a concerted effort to promote their services beyond just the weekend crowds. During the 1950–51 season, they formed the

Beacon Hill Lodge offered a variety of popular après-ski activities to draw skiers to their lodge: ski movies, folk dances and even a heated swimming pool. *Author's collection.*

Donner Summit Winter Sports Committee. The committee was made up of hotel and lift operators situated along fourteen miles of Highway 40. Ernie Nordstrom, longtime Viking Ski Club member and operator of Ski Hi Lodge, was elected president; Jurgen "Red" Vinn, operator of Ski-Inn Lodge, vice president; Charles Van Evera, operator of the rope tows on Beacon Hill, secretary; and Herb Fredericks of the Soda Springs store, treasurer.

They planned a program of day and nighttime skiing and entertainment activities lasting throughout the entire season. Winter visitors could expect ski races, ice skating parties, folk dances, ski movies and even swimming parties at the heated swimming pool at Elmo Moriano's Beacon Hill Lodge. Activities were planned for every night of the week and were posted at all of the Donner Summit resorts to keep guests informed of après-ski happenings. The committee instituted two other innovations to encourage and assist skiers. First, to help reduce congested parking lots, they started a shuttle bus service to transport skiers from their lodge to the slopes. Second, they placed ski attendants at various slopes to assist anyone who needed help. So, "if someone was having trouble with a particular phase of skiing, all they need to do to secure some instruction is to ask the attendant and he will be glad to help out. This free service will be conducted in addition to the actual ski schools."[137] With this plan they hoped to increase midweek visitors and encourage skiers and their families to plan weeklong winter vacations. The committee also hired the San Francisco publicity firm of Lykke-Wilkin and Associates to institute a nationwide publicity program for Donner Summit winter sports.

The city of Auburn was the unofficial gateway to the ski areas along Highway 40. Traveling east, as skiers passed Auburn, the first rope tow was located at Laing's Pioneer Camp, serving a number of intermediate slopes.

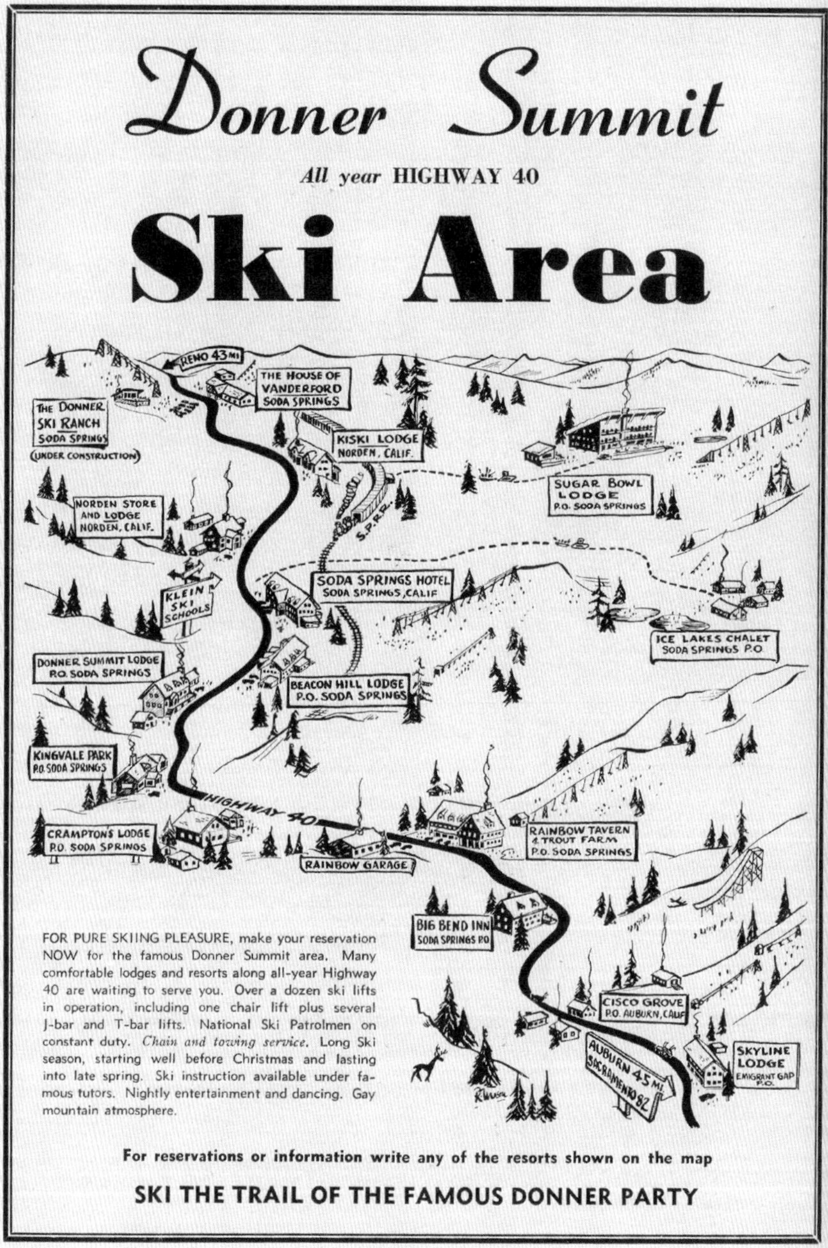

Map showing the numerous lodges and ski tows at Donner Summit, circa 1946. *Author's collection.*

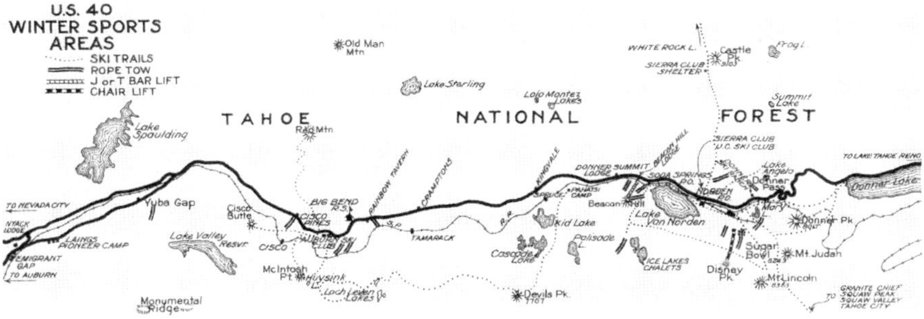

Map showing the location of ski tows along Highway 40, circa 1950. *Author's collection.*

Continuing east, skiers then had their choice of rope tows at Yuba Gap, Cisco Grove and a number of tows at Soda Springs and Norden. The following chapter explores the colorful origins and cast of characters who installed the historic lifts along Highway 40, creating one of California's first and favorite skiing meccas.

Laing's Pioneer Camp

Shortly after the Auburn Ski Club organized in 1929, it began searching for a location that would become its first ski grounds. At that time, traveling east from Sacramento, the farthest one could travel in winter on Highway 40 was Baxter's, so it became the first home of the Auburn Ski Club. It was never outfitted with a tow, but the club built a small ski jump there.

Beyond Baxter's, Laing's Pioneer Camp, located at 5,300 feet elevation, was the first ski center along Highway 40 outfitted with a ski tow. Skiers could travel to the area by car or by Southern Pacific, disembarking at the Emigrant Gap station. An employee from Laing's transported the arriving skiers from the station to the camp by car.

The Laing family enjoyed a long and storied history in the area. Alec and William Laing organized Newcastle Lumber Company in 1912, and William opened the Newcastle Hardware Company in 1923, the two eventually consolidating into a single business. Once the two businesses merged with William at the helm, Alec moved to Carpenter's Flat and began operating Laing's Pioneer Camp as a winter and summer resort in 1933. He developed the resort out of the old Reed Lumber Company buildings that were on the property.

Baxter's never had a ski tow, but it was still popular with skiers. *Author's collection.*

He constructed a ski hill and toboggan slide, and the old millpond was flooded to serve as an ice-skating rink. Skiers could rent skis, skates and toboggans, with meals provided in a large cookhouse.

Laing enlisted the services of Auburn Ski Club president Lane Calder to manage winter activities at the camp. Calder resigned from his Auburn Ski Club presidency in December 1932 so that he could focus his efforts at Laing's.

Laing's became popular with skiers, prompting Laing to make a number of improvements over the years. During the summer of 1935, he added a service station and a ski room. In 1938, he tore down the old mill building that had been used as a group dormitory and later as a garage for cars during heavy snowfall.

He constructed his first ski tow in 1938, a five-hundred-foot rope tow with a two-hundred-foot rise across the meadow, opposite the resort. There were good slopes nearby where beginners through experts could find suitable terrain to improve their skills. The tow also led to a number of prime cross-country ski trails, the finest being an eight-mile trek to Monumental Hill, rewarding the skier with a broad view of the northern Sierra crest. From its summit, skiers could experience a challenging, continuous downhill back to Laing's.

By the 1945–46 season, the rope tow had been lengthened to eight hundred feet, and housekeeping accommodations were available as well. The tow

Left: Laing's Pioneer Camp was outfitted with a rope tow and, most importantly, was accessible by Southern Pacific or by car. *Author's collection.*

Below: Rancho Sierra Inn, circa 1949. Skiers now had their choice of lift served skiing at Laing's or at Rancho Sierra Inn. *Author's collection.*

continued to operate, and when Alec died in 1951, his wife, Nettie, along with their daughter and son-in-law, continued to manage the lodge and ski hill.

In the late 1940s, Laing's was joined by the Rancho Sierra Inn. Built across from Laing's, the inn offered snow play and a rope tow for their skiing guests. To attract and entertain skiers, lodges would often offer special events and programs for après-ski fun. In February 1949, Rancho Sierra Inn showed ski movies. Egil Roed of Norway presented *Classic of Skiing*, featuring Norway's Holmenkollen ski jump, and *Wings to Vikingland*, featuring skiing in Sweden, Denmark and Norway.

Laing's ski tow continued to operate until around 1960. By this time, many of the smaller areas were dying out, especially lodge-operated tows servicing small hills. Skiers had many more areas to choose from, and those that had longer lifts, more vertical feet and more amenities lured them away from the small areas.

Yuba Gap

By the late 1930s, Yuba Gap was becoming a favorite with skiers even though it wasn't outfitted with any tows or lifts. The ski hill was cleared by the Forest Service in 1938, and shortly thereafter, the Big Bend Ranger Station reported that there were 150 cars at the ski hill one weekend day. This popularity eventually led to the construction of a rope tow, and it was in operation by February 1941. In late 1942, ten acres were cleared and graded and a new rope tow was installed. The 750-foot tow, with a 100-foot rise, provided excellent skiing for beginning and intermediate skiers. From the top of the lift, skiers had their choice of a 1,500-foot ride down a number of winding trails.

Shortly after the war, the Adee brothers took over management of Yuba Gap Lodge and the ski lift. Soon after assuming control of the tow, Perry Adee installed floodlights, becoming a pioneer in night skiing. The 1500-watt lights were army surplus and had been used to light airfields. Night skiing was offered on Friday and Saturday nights from 8:00 p.m. to 11:00 p.m. and at other times for special occasions or holidays.

Skiers had all the amenities they needed at the lodge—a warm bed, good meals, ski rentals and very popular tow-served slopes. The Yuba Gap tow continued to operate as late as 1960, but it operated only on weekends and holidays.

After World War II, ski tows proliferated along Highway 40. Yuba Gap Lodge was one of a number of lodges that installed ski tows for the convenience of its skiing guests. *Eastman's Originals Collection. University of California, Davis. General Library. Department of Special Collections.*

Cisco

Today, Cisco is an unexceptional stop along Interstate 80. But for more than thirty years, Cisco was one of Highway 40's most popular winter sports resorts, with throngs of skiers flocking to the area from the 1930s through the 1950s. It was initially home to one of California's best ski jumping hills but was later outfitted with some of the state's first ski tows. Its demise came when I-80 construction went right through the ski grounds, forcing the Auburn Ski Club to move to its current location at Boreal and forcing the other tow operators in the area to either move or shut down their ski tows permanently.

The Auburn Ski Club, founded in 1929, was best known for its world-class ski jumpers and their promotion of the "new" sport of skiing in the 1930s. California skiing was in its infancy at this time, and the club was at the forefront of publicizing and spreading the sport to the masses. Their founder and first president Wendell Robie worked tirelessly to convince the state to keep Highway 40 clear of snow to afford access to ski grounds. And the club hosted some of Northern California's most popular ski meets at Cisco.

Skiers at Cisco, December 1928. Skiing was still in its infancy in California, as evidenced by the ski wear and use of a single pole. *Author's collection.*

After its founding, the club grew rapidly in membership and created facilities that became the envy of ski clubs all over the state. After having to move from their original location at Baxter's, the club dedicated its new ski grounds at Cisco in 1933. In 1934, it was reported, "In the space of a year Robie, acting as a ski-purchaser for his fellow townsmen, bought $2000 worth of skis. Everybody who was anybody wanted to try the thrilling sport. Today more than 30,000 persons avail themselves of the skiing sport at Cisco, about 52 miles from Auburn, and new enthusiasts are being won every day."[138]

The club's rapid rise was attributed in large part to Robie. Dewitt Nelson, longtime Forest Service supervisor, described Robie's personality: "Wendell was a dynamic guy. Anything he went into, he went all the way."[139] It was this drive and enthusiasm from Robie that molded the Auburn Ski Club into one of the largest and most prominent clubs in California.

The focus of ski meets up to the mid-1930s was ski jumping, and the club had some of the best jumpers in the state—and, in Roy Mikkelsen, one of the best jumpers in the nation. But it was common in those days for skiers to be well-rounded, proficient in jumping, downhill skiing, and cross-country skiing. The club had been at the forefront of creating one of

In the 1930s, Cisco was one of Northern California's favorite ski areas. *Author's collection.*

California's best ski jumping hills, and with the introduction of ski tows, it installed one of the first in the country.

The March 29, 1935 issue of the *Ski Bulletin* reported on the principal ski tows in the United States. Six were listed—one in Vermont, four in New Hampshire and the tow at Cisco. It reported, "The Auburn S.C. installed on its hill a 'pull-back', 1,000 feet long, giving a vertical lift of approximately 300 feet. Two double-ended toboggans were rigged so that as one ascended the other descended. *California Ski News* reports that early season difficulties were overcome, and on later week-ends the operation of the pull-back has been highly successful."[140]

These early tows were not without problems and often had to be remodeled or upgraded to prevent breakdowns or improve efficiency. The club arranged for a work party weekend on October 20, 1935, to prepare the upski for the coming season. Lew Holz, Bud Teagarden, Irving Wergeland and Walter Bancrock were in charge of making arrangements for the work party. The tow was outfitted with new sleds, and the California Conservation Corps building was moved adjacent to the new warming hut. The club also completed extensive work on their trails. They cleared more practice runs next to the B jump, widened slopes on the McIntosh trail and cleaned a new trail from the top of Mount McIntosh. This trail went straight down the mountain, making for a very fast descent.

In late 1937, a new and larger electric motor was installed on the tow to accommodate the increased number of skiers expected that season. Johnny Johansen began operating the pull back for the 1937–38 season. The 1937–38 Report of the Winter Sports Committee of the California State Chamber of Commerce documented that there were four ski tows in operation the previous year: a rope tow at Donner Summit, a sled type tow at Yosemite, a J-bar at Cold Springs and the sled tow at Cisco.

The Cisco sled tow was likely modeled after the tow that had been installed at Badger Pass in Yosemite. The continuously operating tow carried passengers on "a double set of large sleighs so connected to an endless cable system that as one sleigh is lifted to the top of Tunnel Mountain, the jump off spot, the other descends to be ready for the next load."[141] Skiers no longer had to make the long, arduous uphill climb to Mount McIntosh. Oliver Kehrlein, ski columnist for the *San Francisco*

The Auburn Ski Club installed the first ski tow at Cisco, a unique sled tow, also called a boat tow. *Courtesy of the Western Skisport Museum.*

The ski facilities at Cisco drew throngs of skiers on the weekends, so parking was sometimes at a premium. The Auburn Ski Club parking area eventually grew to accommodate eight hundred cars. *Author's collection.*

Examiner, wrote, "This lift fortunately placed, makes the McIntosh run practically all down hill both ways."[142]

The December 1938 issue of *Motor Land* reported that the Auburn Ski Club had two power pull backs, as they called them, at Cisco. The sled tow continued to operate at least through 1939. By this time, other types of tows, like the rope tow and J-bar, were becoming more popular, and sled tows would soon become relics of the past. Johansen continued to operate the sled tow and had plans to install a rope tow on nearby smaller slopes.

Cisco was invariably one of the most popular ski destinations on Highway 40 in those days, and by 1938, the area saw much needed improvement to accommodate the increasing crowds, especially on weekends. The parking lot was enlarged, and much work was undertaken to clear slopes of brush and rock, increasing the number of slopes for both beginners and experts.

Once the Auburn Ski Club established ski grounds at Cisco, the wide, clear slopes prompted others to install tows there. In January 1939, Earl Storrs, an electrical engineer, installed a new rope tow that carried skiers to the top of the Class B ski jump. Skiers now had the choice of using the rope tow or the sled tow, which carried sixty persons to the top of Tunnel Mountain every six minutes. Cam Roumage, with an assist from Andy Blodger, began operating an upski at Cisco during the 1940–41 season.

Roumage also operated the Sitzski Lodge at Cisco, so the tow served his guests as well as the general public. His tow was in operation as late as 1960.

The popularity of skiing at Cisco grew even more when the club began offering night skiing in January 1941. The hill was outfitted with floodlights, music and a public address system. Several hundred skiers flocked to the hill for what was likely their first experience skiing at night.

World War II affected the activities of the Auburn Ski Club, but after the war, the club was operating two rope tows: 1,000 feet long with a 300-foot rise and a beginner tow that was 700 feet long with a 100-foot rise. Cam Roumage also made improvements to his ski facilities for the 1945–46 season. He cleared the ski hill to create a wider area that was now served with two tows, 1,800 feet in length. For nonskiers, there was also a toboggan slide, an ash can slide and a warming hut, and Al Halton and his huskies were on hand to provide dogsled rides. Jim Gould operated the store, gas station, housekeeping cabins and ski rentals.

In fall 1949, Tom Vicencio took over operation of Sitzski Lodge. Roumage gave up his resort so that he could focus on other business ventures. The deal consisted of a lease on the resort, which included a forty-bed dormitory, coffee shop, kitchen and two rope tows. Vicencio was anxious to have a successful 1949–50 season, so he began making improvements, clearing runs of brush and rocks and improving tow capacity. He also hoped to increase membership in the Sitzski Club and create package deals for youth groups.

Big changes took place in preparation for the 1955–56 season. Wayne Poulsen (president), Roy Mikkelsen (vice president), Pete Johnson (sports director), Orrin Ellingsen and several other skiers formed the Snowshoe Corporation in 1955. The group leased the Auburn Ski Club grounds to operate as a commercial enterprise and renamed the area Cisco Tunnel Mountain.

The grand opening was held on December 17–18, 1955. Three lifts were in operation to inaugurate the Snowshoe Corporation's new area: a 1,295-foot-long Poma lift with a 443-foot rise that carried skiers to the top of Tunnel Mountain and two rope tows. The Poma lift, with a capacity of seven hundred skiers per hour, was the first Poma lift on Highway 40. A second lift, a 500-foot platter lift imported by Hannes Schroll, was installed and in operation for the 1957–58 season. After these improvements, it was claimed that it was "one of the most complete winter sports areas in the Sierras. It will open this season with two new lifts, two refurbished lodges, including a large modern lunch room and a large warming house and expert ski instruction."[143]

Above: The Auburn Ski Club developed Cisco into one of the finest, best-equipped ski areas on Highway 40. *Author's collection.*

Left: Advertisement for Sitzski Lodge at Cisco, circa 1950. *Author's collection.*

Enthusiasm about the improvements and the area ran high, as Johnson commented,

> *Ski Cisco will become a by-word to Northern California skiers and skiers-to-be because of its facilities, its accessibility and the variety of its slopes. But foremost, Cisco at Tunnel Mountain will be a resort area where the skiers feel "at home," where everyone is welcome, families encouraged to participate in our outdoor activities and clubs encouraged and assisted in running their races and meets—all within easy vision of our two tremendous sun porches.*[144]

Cisco Tunnel Mountain operated until the late 1950s. For years, the state had been making major improvements along Highway 40. A new section of freeway was opened between Hampshire Rocks and Soda Springs in November 1959, and there were plans to realign the freeway and add lanes in other areas, including Cisco. These road improvements cut right through the ski grounds. With money it received from the state, the Auburn Ski Club purchased property for its current location at Boreal. Some of the other ski lodges and equipment were auctioned off in summer 1960. Portions of land that had been acquired for freeway construction from Emigrant Gap to Hampshire Rocks needed to be cleared. A notice for the auction stated, "Ski lodge and residence, one-story building, public address system, and outdoor lighting, located across the river from the Standard station at Cisco Grove, and formerly owned by John B. White. Minimum acceptable bid is $85."[145]

Cisco had served Northern California skiers for more than twenty-five years, becoming one of the most developed and modern California ski areas at that time. Cisco had everything a 1930s skier could want—ski jumps for all abilities, wide, clear slopes to serve all skill levels, a warming hut, ski tows and ample parking. The Auburn Ski Club led the way and set the standard for ski area development when skiing in California was in its infancy. The club is still thriving today, focusing on developing Olympic-caliber skiers in both alpine and cross-country skiing.

Pla-vada Hills

Pla-vada Hills was located at Kingvale on Highway 40, four miles west of Soda Springs at an elevation of 6,100 feet. It opened during the 1956–57 season under the management of Dick Read and was outfitted with a 550-foot rope tow with a vertical rise of 175 feet. It also had a coffee shop, a lounge and a two-hundred-car parking lot.

For the 1959–60 season, Pla-vada was advertised as the "new improved Pla-vada Hills."[146] A new T-bar had been installed, carrying up to six hundred skiers per hour to the top of the intermediate slope. The highway had been realigned in 1959, resulting in the beginner hill becoming two hundred feet closer to the highway and the rope tow lengthened to about nine hundred feet. The chalet was moved about one thousand feet and was now beside the Highway 40 exit. To round out the area, there was a ski shop, a snack bar, plenty of parking and certified ski instructors. Jim Campbell Jr. managed the area at this time, and Don Kast was the director of the Far West Ski Instructors Association–certified ski school.

By the 1963–64 season, Pla-vada was owned by the Nicholls Estate Company, best known for its involvement in mining. Knowing they couldn't compete with the larger areas at higher elevations farther up the highway, the management promoted their greatest asset, the bunny hills for beginners. They also made a number of improvements for the 1963–64 season, the most significant being the new terrain opened up by moving a power line and installing a new tow. With these improvements, the area drew more skiers that season, and management hoped that Pla-vada would have a chairlift installed and running for the following season.

The chairlift never became a reality, but they operated two rope tows, a platter lift, and a T-bar. Pla-vada became known as a first-class family resort and was the closest to Bay Area and Sacramento skiers.

In the mid-1970s, there was a cluster of resorts on or near Interstate 80: Pla-vada, Boreal Ridge, Soda Springs, Donner Ski Ranch, and Sugar Bowl. Pla-vada was the lowest in elevation and was overshadowed by its much larger neighbors. It was known as a beginners' area and was a perfect place for new skiers who were intimidated by larger or more crowded slopes.

Unable to compete with areas that had more snow and more varied terrain, Pla-vada closed in late 1973 but opened for business for a short time in November 1974. It was closed permanently after that.

Today's skiers can find superb skiing and reliable snow a short distance away at Donner Ski Ranch, Sugar Bowl and Soda Springs ski areas. The old Pla-vada Hills slopes are still visible as one exits Highway 80. It has been operating as a snow play area called Kingvale Recreational Resort for a number of years, with the old ski runs making for an ideal snow play operation. The area sold in August 2017 and was again listed for sale as of

Above: Long before Pla-vada Hills Ski Area opened in 1956–57, its location directly adjacent to Highway 40 made it a popular stop with skiers. *Author's collection.*

Left: Advertisement promoting the new T-bar and other amenities at Pla-vada Hills. *Author's collection.*

Pla-vada's deserted ski slopes, now used for snow play, are dotted with the remains of old ski lifts. *Author's collection.*

The upper terminal of one of Pla-vada's ski lifts still stands, circa 2018. *Author's collection.*

November 2019. The 297-acre property has multiple possible uses: sledding and tubing, snowmobiling in winter and ATVs in summer, a zip line, bike trails and a wedding venue. Its days as a ski resort ended more than forty years ago, joining the annals of Tahoe and Donner lost ski areas.

Rainbow Tavern

In its heyday, Rainbow Tavern was one of the most popular resorts between Auburn and Lake Tahoe. It is located at a beautiful site near the Yuba River and was popular in both winter and summer. Herstle Jones purchased the original Tavern building in 1932 and continued to make improvements and additions to it over the years. He added a trout farm and electric plant to furnish electricity to nearby cabins. In 1934, there were accommodations for twenty guests, and a January 17, 1934 *Oakland Tribune* advertisement said it "affords comforts of a palatial chalet."

After investing an estimated $50,000 for improvements, Jones held a grand opening on December 14, 1935. The capacity more than doubled to accommodate seventy people, and every room was steam heated and furnished with a private bath. Over the years, some of the Donner area's best instructors were hired to provide ski lessons at the tavern. The first was Auburn Ski Club ace Johnny Johansen, followed by Peter Picard and Edvi Aro.

In fall 1938, a 1,250-foot J-bar was installed behind the tavern. The tow opened up acres of untracked country above the lodge in addition to a slalom run and a longer two-mile trail back to the bottom.

Jones was ready to move on to other business ventures, so in March 1944, he sold the tavern to John S. Flagg, a San Francisco building contractor. The purchase price was reported to be about $150,000. Two years later, Flagg sold the area for more than $200,000. Flagg and his brother A.J. Flagg decided to assume an option on the 265-room Tahoe Tavern.

J.J. Navone and Lawrence Curtola purchased Rainbow Tavern from Flagg in spring 1946. The change in ownership took place officially on March 1, and the new owners immediately began formulating plans for additional lodge facilities and improvements to the ski hill. Navone and Curtola had extensive experience in the resort business and were well qualified to expand and improve on the area. They enlisted Hannes Bernard to provide ski lessons at the J-bar.

Above: Skiers could usually find ample snow on the slopes behind Rainbow Tavern. *Author's collection.*

Left: Skiers at Rainbow Tavern had access to the J-bar right outside their door. *Author's collection.*

Rainbow Tavern, circa 2018. The ski lifts have been gone since the 1960s, but in its heyday, it was one of the most popular ski lodges along Highway 40. *Author's collection.*

However, Navone and Curtola didn't own the property for long. W.W. "Tiny" Naylor purchased the area in fall 1946 for a price of $250,000. Naylor had started a waffle shop in Reno in the 1930s that eventually led to a string of restaurants throughout California. Naylor had two partners assisting in the business, A.A. Mercola and D.A. Hansen. In April 1949, Hansen, who had been managing the resort, took over full ownership. The tavern continued to change hands over the years, with Brant Chaplin assuming ownership in early 1951 and Milt and Maggie Avila taking over in 1956.

Avila was operating a new rope tow by January 1957. Then, in November 1957, he graded and removed rocks, creating more open slopes, removed the J-bar and installed a new 1,785-foot Poma lift. He hoped these upgrades would attract some of the skiers on their way to Donner Summit areas, especially when blizzard conditions made travel difficult or resulted in road closures.

Avila began hosting weekly Sunday slaloms he dubbed Pot-of-Gold races. He and ski instructor Grats Powers formed the Alpin Ski School, with Powers teaching at Donner Ski Ranch and Avila holding down the instructor duties at Rainbow. Both resorts also had a complete ski shop on site, the Alpinhaus.

Skiing at Rainbow Tavern continued until about 1962. By February 1963, the Avilas were owners of Glacier Gap Lodge, located around the bend from Rainbow Tavern, and continued to own and operate the Alpinhaus Ski Shop. Once the Avilas sold their interest in the tavern, it spelled the end of the ski tow operation. There were larger and better ski areas elsewhere on the summit, so Rainbow Tavern's days as a ski area came to an end.

HOUSE OF VANDERFORD'S AND HOYFJELLET LODGE

The *San Francisco Examiner* announced the December 1937 opening of the House of Vanderford's: "On the Donner Pass road, a new center has been developed at the summit, elevation 7,316 feet. The Vanderford's have built a rest house with accommodations for 25 week-enders and a lunchroom for transients. Johnny Ellis will be in charge of skiing and give instructions."[147]

The three-story lodge was located across from the future Donner Ski Ranch and adjacent to the slopes of what would later be developed as Sugar Bowl Ski Area. Vanderford's added a tow to the lodge in January 1938 and added a new tow in January 1942. "Ma" Vanderford, as owner Jessie Vanderford was called, became renowned for her lodge's home-away-from-home atmosphere.

Johnny Ellis began working at Vanderford's shortly after it opened and became its first instructor. Some of the summit's best instructors taught there over the years, including Johnny Johansen, Fred Klein and Bill Strickland.

In October 1937, Ellis wrote,

> *I am enthusiastic for the coming winter. My closest associates will evidently be Mr. and Mrs. Vanderford, who are now boarding me and whose dining room, store and a projected garage, and living accommodations for skiers—all fit in with my ski hill development. Mr. Vanderford is an old rail-road man.... They have been building up their place here, Mr. Vanderford doing his own building for four years and are just this year beginning to round it into a working outfit. They are very nice people, likable, and I think, personally attractive and adaptable to a ski crowd. I doubt if they realize what a powerful lobbyist I'll be in their affairs this winter. But I intend this summit to be a place of mighty good times for a real ski crowd and shan't be bashful about trying to make it so. I think we'll do it together.*[148]

VANDERFORD'S DONNER SUMMIT SKI LODGE

HOTEL ACCOMMODATIONS - DINING ROOM - UP-SKI

TELEGRAPH VANDERFORD'S NORDEN, CALIF. • RENTAL SKI EQUIPMENT • FRED KLEIN, SKI INSTRUCTOR CLASS & PRIVATE

Top: House of Vanderford's (*bottom right*) was surrounded by prime ski terrain that would later be developed as Donner Ski Ranch and Sugar Bowl ski areas. *Courtesy of Donner Summit Historical Society, Norm Sayler Collection.*

Bottom: Advertisement for Vanderford's, promoting their up-ski and ski instructor Fred Klein. *Author's collection.*

In its almost six years of existence, Vanderford's played a central role to skiing on the summit. When it opened in December 1937, it was one of the few lodges available to skiers on the summit. And as skier numbers increased, ski injuries increased. The American Red Cross began to provide first aid courses for skiers and set up first aid stations at various locations along Highway 40. Vanderford's was one of those stations and had most of the equipment necessary to provide proper care to injured skiers.

Left: Vanderford's was one of the most popular lodges on the summit. Jessie Vanderford treated skiers like family, earning her the nickname "Ma" Vanderford. *Courtesy of Donner Summit Historical Society, Norm Sayler Collection.*

Below: Hoyfjellet Lodge as it looks today. In the 1950s, John Zahara operated two rope tows for his skiing guests. *Courtesy of Gigi Heckendorn.*

Business was severely reduced during the war, but Vanderford's catered to the soldiers who were stationed in the area. Johnny Johansen borrowed skis from a local ski shop and gave free weekend ski lessons to the soldiers who were guarding the Southern Pacific rail line.

In September 1944, the House of Vanderford was destroyed by fire. At that time, it had been leased to the Morrison-Knudsen Company, whose employees were conducting railroad work in the area. Fifty-five men had been housed at the lodge. The fire marked the end of Vanderford's, one of the most popular ski lodges on the summit.

Just down the road from Vanderford's, near the Central Sierra Snow Lab, stands Hoyfjellet Lodge. Hoyfjellet translates to "high mountain location." John Zaraha started building Hoyfjellet Lodge in the early 1930s. It began with one room and a loft, but he soon found it was too small to accommodate the number of visitors who wanted to stay at his lodge. Because of the demand, Zahara built additions to the lodge over the years. The 5,500-square-foot lodge was built with stone from the surrounding mountains and timber from the snow sheds. In the 1950s, he installed and operated two rope tows. In 1960, he sold the lodge to Cy and Missie Maughan of San Jose. The Maughans owned the lodge until 1975, when Corky and Gigi Heckendorn purchased it. They still own and operate it today. No ski tows operate there now, but skiers are within a one-mile radius of Donner Summit's three ski areas—Soda Springs Ski Area, Donner Ski Ranch and Sugar Bowl.

ICE LAKES CHALET–SERENE LAKES CLUB

Serene Lakes (elevation 7,200 feet) is situated near the top of Donner Summit, ninety-eight miles east of Sacramento and forty-one miles west of Reno. Mark Twain originally gave the lakes their true names—Serena and Dulzura—but they became known as Ice Lakes when the Central Pacific Railway began cutting ice from the lakes for their refrigeration cars and for the city of San Francisco.

Recreational enterprises at Serene Lakes underwent a number of name changes and transformations over the years. The first operation began in January 1939 and was named the Ice Lakes Club. The founders, made up of a group of businessmen and prominent skiers, modeled it after the famous Lake Placid Club in New York. It would provide winter and summer activities for its select members, which would be limited to five hundred life and five hundred regular members. Club secretary M. Corey spelled out the plan for the group:

> *We have lots of beautiful beach and city clubs, but where can we find an exclusive, modern mountain club in Northern California? Our present plans are to build this Spring a comfortable but moderate priced clubhouse large enough to accommodate the membership and which we can operate at city prices. It will have the necessary facilities for skiers, a dining room where moderate priced meals can be obtained, a cocktail bar and all accommodations found in a first-class hotel. Because of the patronage of our members, we believe that we will be able to offer first-class accommodations at greatly reduced rates to members. It will be strictly a members' club, and we are also making provisions for members who may later desire to build their own cabins.*[149]

Membership in the club was by application only and had to be approved by the membership committee. It was felt that "This committee, consisting of many ardent skiers, assures the development of the club in the best interests of the skiing fraternity."[150] In addition to business owners and other professionals, the makeup of the inaugural membership committee was a virtual who's who of Northern California skiers: Roy Mikkelsen, Bill and Fred Klein, Martin Arrouge, Wayne Poulsen and Charles Van Evera. There were a handful of ski tows operating on Donner Summit at this time, but it would be seven more years before Serene Lakes had its own tow.

The advent of World War II brought future development of the club to a standstill. But, once the war was over, interest in Serene Lakes as a private club was revived. In June 1945, the Ice Lakes Chalet corporation was formed. F.H. Thorinson of San Francisco purchased several hundred acres of land from Dr. and Mrs. J.G. Mackay of Auburn and Alice and Nina Haman of Roseville for $30,000. Thorinson then conveyed the property to the corporation. Other directors of the corporation were Lloyd Sundberg, George Sundell, Alex A. Johnson and Vernon Holmes, all of San Francisco. The articles of incorporation stated that their purpose was to "operate tourist and vacation resorts."[151]

There was lodging for fifty in housekeeping cabins and visitors were treated to a two-mile scenic ride in an army-surplus Weasel to get to the chalet from the Southern Pacific station. Thorinson installed the first ski lift at the chalet, a 1,200-foot-long rope tow with a 400-foot rise. Located to the west of the lakes, it began operating in time for the 1946–47 season, and Merle Tobias was charged with operating the lift.

Above: Ice Lakes Chalet in the 1940s. The first ski tow was installed by F.H. Thorinson and began operating during the 1946–47 season. *Courtesy of Donner Summit Historical Society, Norm Sayler Collection.*

Left: Brochure promoting Thorinson's Ice Lakes Chalet, prominently featuring skiing on the cover. *Author's collection.*

In December 1949, Colonel Bill Rutherford, a longtime resident of the area with extensive experience in the hotel business, took over Ice Lakes Chalet. In January 1951, large crowds flocked to the chalet for night skiing, one of three areas (Cisco and Yuba Gap Lodge also had lighted slopes) along Highway 40 that offered night skiing.

The next chapter in Serene Lakes ski history began in the late 1950s. Frank A. Allen and his wife took over Ice Lakes Chalet and renamed it Sierra Lakes Club. The Sierra Lakes Club was a private organization to be made up of 2,500 families that planned to promote the area as a private club. Allen hired some of the best and most experienced men on the summit. Norm Sayler was chosen as the new assistant manager in charge of clearing ski runs and installing lifts. Jerry Mikacich was on the recreation staff for both winter and summer seasons. Jim Winthers had an advisory role in recreation, and Johnny Johansen was part of the construction crew.

Excitement ran high at the prospect of a four-season private resort. In 1959, Bill Strickland wrote,

> *Can you picture, for example, the keen anticipation you, as a ski club member, can have toward a day or week of skiing, knowing that participants will be limited to members only, knowing that there will never be a lift line, knowing that you'll never be confronted with a lack of parking area. Knowing that you'll be able to ski with people you've known for years, because they too are members—and best of all, knowing that the facilities will be there and available to you, without congestion from now on, for all year use because membership will be curtailed to a workable maximum.*[152]

In May 1959, Allen submitted a request to the county supervisors requesting that the road into Serene Lakes be paved. The construction of five hundred summer homes could be started once the road leading to the area was improved. The board denied the request, stating that there were other projects in the county that took priority over the road.

In spite of the road decision, the Allens were given approval for a five-hundred-lot subdivision in April 1960. Their plans were much more extensive than the clubs that preceded them. They planned for a shopping center, golf course, ski lifts, lodge, swimming pool, stables, campground and trailer park, and they expected the project to be finished in 1963. Norm Sayler, former owner of Donner Ski Ranch and Donner Summit historian, recalled, "I went

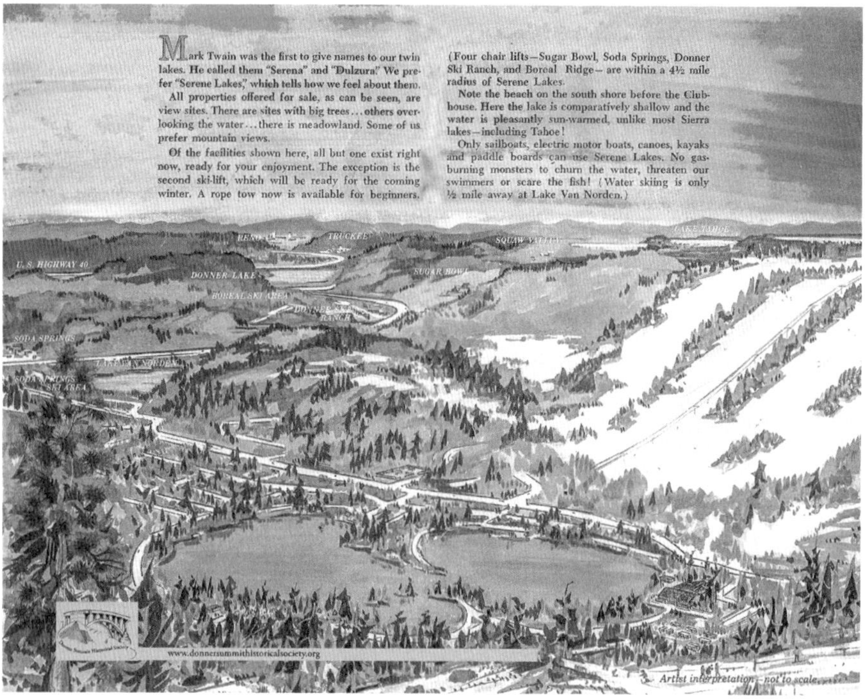

Artist's depiction of the Sierra Lakes Club and the planned ski area that was never realized. *Courtesy of Donner Summit Historical Society, Norm Sayler Collection.*

to work for Allen in 1960. I cut two chairlift lines on Rowton Peak. They were going to install two chairlifts and I was going to leave Donner Ski Ranch and go to work for them. The money didn't come through to build the chairlifts."[153]

The dreams and aspirations of the Sierra Lakes Club never came to be realized, and the organization disbanded in summer 1966. Serene Lakes did not lie unnoticed for long. The property was taken over by S.V.H. Investments, headed by S.V. Hunsaker. The deal included four square miles and two forty-acre lakes. Membership included the use of the facilities at the lakes, clubhouse and a winter sports area. There were paved county roads leading to each lot, something that Allen's Sierra Lakes Club couldn't accomplish.

The new owners immediately made improvements for its skiing members, adding a T-bar during the 1966–67 season. The 650-foot lift, situated east of the clubhouse, serviced a beginners' slope and operated on the weekends. Members of the Serene Lakes Club were instrumental in getting the T-bar up and running. The February 1967 issue of *Serene Lakes News* reported,

Serene Lakes ski hill outfitted with a rope tow. This tow operated on a hill above the current recreational beach. *Courtesy of Bill Oudegeest.*

> *Helmut Schlitzer, San Francisco, an electrical technician, translated the directions that came with the equipment; all were in German. Fred Wallin, Sunnyvale, whose cabin is on Lake Drive, also worked on the electrical system and bravely volunteered to test the lift. Lou Berinti, Sacramento, dug out at least four 6' holes after a storm, so that pads could be constructed to anchor guy lines.*[151]

It is unknown how long the ski tows operated at Serene Lakes. Club members had the luxury of private, secluded ski slopes for those looking for an uncrowded, relaxed skiing experience. They were also fortunate to have the choice of prime ski areas nearby: Donner Ski Ranch, Sugar Bowl and Soda Springs Ski Area.

HILLTOP–TRUCKEE WINTER SPORTS PARK

Hilltop, located in the town of Truckee, is historic for a number of reasons. It had the first mechanical ski lift in the nation and was the scene of the first winter carnival in the West. And it became California's first winter sports center. The only way to cross the Sierra in winter prior to the 1930s was by train, so the first ski areas naturally developed near Southern Pacific tracks. Truckee also had hotels and restaurants that could serve winter visitors from Sacramento, San Francisco and nearby Reno. The winter access and availability of lodging led to Truckee becoming California's first winter sports center.

Winter carnivals or "The Fiesta of the Snows" as they were sometimes called began in 1896. Events were held at the Ice Palace, but jumping and tobogganing took place at Hilltop. The first tow at Hilltop was a toboggan lift installed in 1910. According to Mort Lund, this was the only ski tow operating in the United States in 1929. Lund wrote, "It lay on the snow, a wire cable with hooks attached, a haulback tow pulling mostly toboggans and a few skiers."[155] That was three years before a rope tow was patented in Zurich, Switzerland.

The winter carnivals struggled in the early years and were held intermittently, but by the 1930s, ski trains, dubbed Snowball Specials, were bringing winter visitors from Sacramento, the Bay Area and Reno. Ski jump meets became a weekend highlight of the carnivals, but the popularity of ski jumping eventually waned as mechanized ski tows ushered in the popularity of downhill skiing.

The Snowball Specials provided all-important winter transportation for Reno, Sacramento and Bay Area skiers. *Author's collection.*

Truckee skiing became more organized with the formation of the Truckee Ski Club on December 22, 1914. There had been talk in previous years among skiers and outdoor enthusiasts regarding the formation of a club, but nothing ever materialized. Everyone was urged to join the club, man, woman or child and skiers and nonskiers alike. A one-dollar fee was charged to defray the expense of medals, badges and so forth. Also, at this first meeting, the club arranged to award medals for the first cross-country race to be held in California.

The organization of the club included the election of officers, formation of bylaws and preparations for new members. The officers were pioneer California ski jumper Irving Klepp, president; T.J. O'Hanrahan, vice president; Harrison Fox, secretary; B.A. Cassidy, treasurer; Skiwart[156] Lieutenant William Hiller, holder of many medals from Switzerland; and William B. Gelatt, as one of the directors.

The Truckee Ski Club operated sporadically over the years and was later replaced by the Truckee Outing Club. The outing club was formed on November 8, 1935, during a meeting of the Truckee Chamber of Commerce. Letters of incorporation were filed in February 1936. C.B. White, president of the chamber of commerce, appointed W.M. Englehart to lead the club and its fifteen directors.

Through the efforts of the Truckee Chamber of Commerce and the Truckee Outing Club, Truckee had grown to be a popular winter sports center. After the 1936–37 season, the members discussed improvements they wanted to make for the following year. Their first priority was to complete a new ice palace. They also discussed the possibility of installing a ski tow, replacing the current toboggan slide and building new ski jumps on a nearby hill so that the club could host ski meets and bid for a state meet. They had never been awarded a state meet because club facilities were not up to standard.

By fall 1938, in spite of the chamber's ambitious plans, many Truckee merchants no longer wanted to fund local winter sports. The *Sierra Sun and Truckee Republican* reported, "Unless Truckee interests rule otherwise during the immediate future, efforts will be made to dispose of winter sports as a civic enterprise and the equipment, grounds and the other assets turned over to private interests." The paper added, "It was pointed out that despite the favorable reports by many of the local establishments, which benefit annually from the influx of the snow sport enthusiasts, that others, who may or may not have benefited have turned thumbs down on the prospect with refusals to assist in a financial way."[157] A committee, made up of Frank S. Powell, Lotta Bryant and C.E. Smith, was formed to interview merchants and others to determine the course of action the chamber would take. The chamber was reluctant to abandon what was perhaps Truckee's most valuable winter asset, but it was the membership of the chamber that would determine whether they would continue to financially back the activities.

The "no" vote came in, so Truckee winter sports would no longer be supported by the local chamber of commerce. Soon thereafter, three offers were made by private parties to take over the concession. The proposals were presented at the November 14, 1938 chamber of commerce meeting. The first proposal came from Orland Sanders, representing eighteen Truckee youth who were anxious to keep the skating rink in use. The second offer came from Earl Edmunds and Stanford Gregory. Their plan was to assume responsibility for the skating rink, ski grounds, buildings and other related equipment. The third proposition came from three Reno men who wanted to lease the rink, skates and other equipment and operate it as a business.

C.B. White, director of the chamber of commerce as well as the president of the Truckee Outing Club, "called a meeting of the directors of the chamber of commerce to take definite steps, but suggested that the matter also be thrashed out at a meeting of the outing club held at the California restaurant Monday night. The three plans were presented at the latter meeting without any concrete results, the final decision being referred to the chamber directors."[158]

The directors of the chamber of commerce met again on November 22, 1938, and it was determined that the administration and equipment of Truckee's winter sports be turned over to Earl Edmunds and Stanford Gregory. The pair submitted a plan to assume the responsibilities involved in keeping Truckee's winter sports operating. Edmunds said that "they planned to operate the rink and other concessions on a commercial basis, paying their own expenses and maintaining the equipment."[159]

Edmunds and Stanford successfully directed winter sports activities during the 1938–39 season and were again meeting with the chamber in September 1939 to request they continue with the operation for the 1939–40 season. The September 14, 1939 *Sierra Sun and Truckee Republican* reported that the chamber did not have the authority to turn over the facilities to anyone, but the directors were hoping to have the pair oversee the concession again.

Apparently, the chamber could not come to a resolution regarding Truckee's facilities, so organized winter sports did not take place during the 1939–40 season. By February 1940, several local men had expressed interest in taking over the operation. Dan D. Smith and Jack Wolert, Truckee building contractor, knew the legal challenges they faced, but met with the directors of the Truckee Public Utility District (PUD) on February 27, 1940, to argue their case.

Smith claimed he had sufficient support to operate as a community project, while Wolert wanted to run the concession as a private enterprise. PUD director Ben Tonini planned to call a meeting of local business owners to get a majority vote between the two proposals.

With the town seeking a permanent solution to winter sports management, the Truckee Outing Club reorganized in May 1940. Yell Nobles, a Truckee bank manager, was elected president, succeeding R.W. Siebold. C.J. Bowers was the new vice president; Vernon E. Pearson, secretary; and C.B. White, treasurer. It was hoped that the club could assume the organization and promotion of Truckee winter sports. Plans were created to work on the hill during the summer and fall, and District Forest Ranger Hobart I. Snider made arrangements for the transfer or trade of the property, furthering the opportunity for a permanent winter sports program at Hilltop.

Excitement ran high after that organizational meeting. The *Sierra Sun and Truckee Republican* reported, "In preparation for one of the most concerted membership drives and promotional campaigns in the winter sports history of Truckee, more than a score of members of the revamped Truckee Outing Club met last week at the fire station to elect officers and outline plans for the future."[160]

Starting in July 1940, the club hoped to secure three hundred members through an ambitious membership drive. It was also the first time (excepting the toboggan tow) that plans were made to outfit Hilltop with a motor-driven tow. Preparing the hill and installing the tow would be a financial challenge for the club, but they hoped the increased membership would offset some of the expense. The club was anxious to install the tow, so at a meeting on July 30, 1940, they voted to proceed with plans for the tow even though the membership drive had just begun. C.B. White, C.J. Bowers and R.S. Boren were tasked with the purchase and preparation of the equipment.

It was soon realized that the club would not be able to finance the tow or operate the concession, so in August, the Truckee PUD agreed to provide financial assistance to make Truckee's much-needed ski tow a reality. "C.B. White, Laurence Owens and Dick Joseph appeared before the directors to make the application in behalf of the outing club. It was assured that the treasury of the district will not suffer and that the assistance must be considered in the form of community promotion which will naturally increase the revenues of the district to offset the amounts offered."[161]

So, the struggles that began during the 1938–39 season to find an individual or group to oversee Truckee winter sports were finally over. Private citizens and the Truckee Outing Club had made attempts to take over the concession, but it proved too legally and financially challenging for them to succeed. Hilltop had shifted from the financial support of chamber of commerce members to Truckee PUD funding. With the combined efforts of the Truckee PUD and the Truckee Outing Club, the tow would soon become a dream realized.

In late August 1940, the Truckee Outing Club began raising the $2,500 needed for the tow. The Truckee PUD contributed $1,000 toward the project. The club submitted the projected costs for the tow: motor, $200; rope, $275;

installation, $425; power lines, $425; repairs to scaffold, $200; repairs to pavilion, $300; and clearing the hill and operating reserve, $625.

Dan D. Smith, along with Mrs. William Johnson, spent ten days soliciting funds for the development of the ski facilities. He gathered $950, noting that "in nearly every instance Truckee people were vitally interested in the proposed program and were willing to contribute toward its fulfillment."[162]

Once the funds were secured, work progressed rapidly. A number of Truckee men spent every weekend clearing brush and preparing the hill for the tow. Surveys of the area had been completed by mid-September, and installation of the lift was set to begin soon. At a meeting on September 24, the club voted to purchase approximately fifty acres of land from O.C. Haslett. This additional acreage was needed for the installation of the tow and related equipment.

Work continued through October, and by the end of the month, the fifteen-horsepower motor and other equipment, except the 3,200 feet of rope, had arrived and was being installed. A former office building of the Works Progress Administration had been moved to house the motor and other equipment.

The hill was almost ready by the end of November. The first payment on the property had been made, the scaffold and pavilion had been repaired and work on the tow house had been completed. "The 15-horsepower electric motor with its required equipment has been installed and a line has been run from a terminal near the Truckee River to the motor shed.

Historic Hilltop finally outfitted with its first ski tow, December 1940. *Author's collection.*

From the upper slopes at Hilltop, skiers had a bird's-eye view of the base area and ski jump. *Author's collection.*

The up-ski run has been cleared of brush and trees and ski runs are now being prepared for the first snow."[163]

The rope finally arrived, and the club was busy with its installation in mid-December. After months of fundraising and preparation, the tow began operation during the last week of December 1940, under the direction of C.J. Bowers. It worked smoothly and safely, carrying skiers 1,500 feet at a speed of seven miles per hour. The Truckee Outing Club named the new area Truckee Winter Sports Park. This was the fourteenth ski tow operating on Highway 40 between Emigrant Gap and Truckee.

Big crowds flocked to the tow during its first season, and it continued to attract skiers over the years, but by summer 1944, the Truckee PUD was considering the sale of the ski grounds and facilities. "It is proposed to sell the 70 acres of park grounds, the pavilion, up-ski equipment and scaffold to private owners who will agree to continue operation of the site as a winter and summer recreational park. Edmunds pointed out many advantages to be gained under proper ownership, picturing the pine-studded play ground as a model location for all sorts of recreational facilities."[164]

In the years immediately after the war, Hilltop's history becomes a little sketchy. It was reported that Charles A. Tollefsen purchased the area in December 1945, and the *Skier's Handbook 1947* states that Tollefsen was operating a 1,300-foot rope tow during the 1946–47 season.[165] However, another source reports that in December 1945, Truckee Winter Sports Park was sold to Emery M. Carter of Los Angeles and Ed S. Crandall of Oakland. They had already taken possession of the area and were completing construction of a dormitory. Carter and Crandall are credited with renaming the area Hilltop. They also enlisted two of Truckee's pioneer ski instructors, George "Bud" Zorich and Frank L. Titus, to open and operate a ski school. They added a ski shop and a second rope tow on the lower part of the hill. The 300-foot-long lower tow started 150 feet from the lodge and connected with a 1,600-foot tow, which led to many expert trails. The area was still popular and used frequently for ski jumping until the scaffold was torn down in 1950.

In any case, it appears that both Tollefsen and the Crandall brothers were involved in owning and managing Hilltop in the mid-1940s, and the Crandalls operated it for a number of years until they moved to Los Angeles in the mid-1950s. The area fell into disrepair, the old rope tow turned to rust and the historic area lay dormant. The Truckee PUD took over briefly in 1959 and initially considered leasing the property. But it soon decided to list the property for sale. There were two stipulations: the seventy acres had to be used for recreational purposes and a minimum bid of $51,000 was required. Harry and Zella Herzog were the only bidders, and the sale was approved on June 30, 1959. Herzog, a motel owner and real estate man, immediately began installing a new Poma lift and making other improvements.

Advertisement for Harry Herzog's new Poma lift and rope tows at Hilltop Lodge. *Author's collection.*

Herzog's newly remodeled Hill Top Lodge opened on December 31, 1959. The lodge now had a cocktail lounge, cafeteria and dining room with a gift shop and ski shop. A new 160-bed dormitory had also been recently completed. Herzog hired Eugene Stark and his wife to manage the area. The 2,200-foot Poma lift began operating on January 2, 1960. They also installed a 400-foot rope tow for beginners.

The Poma lift and rope tow continued to operate through the 1960s, but only on the weekends. During the 1970s, area ownership changed twice. In the early

The lower terminal of the old Poma lift still stands at the base of Hilltop. *Author's collection.*

Lift towers and other relics still adorn the slopes at Hilltop, marking a history of more than one hundred years of skiing at Truckee. *Author's collection.*

1970s, Mr. and Mrs. Robert Kent operated Hilltop Lodge along with the Poma lift and rope tow. Danny West and Rick Kent handled the ski school duties.

Then, in 1976, Frederick Kohler was looking for a challenging business enterprise. He commented, "I happened through Truckee, inquired around and found myself at Hilltop."[166] Kohler was not interested in operating the ski area, so the tows stopped operating permanently at the end of 1976.

By the early 2000s, the fifty-three-acre hilltop property was targeted for development. The plan, as it was proposed in 2004, "would create a village on the northern portion of the hilltop, with three new restaurants, ski hill condominiums, a Bed and Breakfast, and more than 40,000 square feet of retail space. Directly behind the village, 80 rental apartments would be constructed. Commercial, lodging and multi-family housing would flank the village to the east. To the south, workforce housing, multi-family and single family homes would be constructed."[167]

It was critical that the developers and town planners come up with a plan that would honor the history of the site as well as present the best use of the site for the town's needs. The plan was revised over the years, with the 2008 version better representing and preserving the importance of the historic ski hill.

Hilltop still lies vacant today. The historic acreage is for sale, real estate signs placed prominently at the bottom of the old ski slope. The sale includes "43.8 acres of prime development land situated in the center of the highly regarded, historic Hilltop site, perched directly above Truckee's Commercial Row and the beautiful Truckee River. The site offers a rich history, a superior location, and a Town approved masterplan for development on the site."[168] The Cottonwood Restaurant operates in the old lodge, and the hill is dotted with remnants of the old Truckee Winter Sports Park. Its appearance today belies the important skiing history of the location and the historic ski jumping meets that once took place there.

NOTES

Introduction

1. Gillis, "Tunnels of the Pacific Railroad," 156–57.
2. "Winter Sports Promotion California State Chamber," *Ski Illustrated*, December/January 1937–38, 36.
3. Berry and Wentworth, *Lost Sierra*, 185.
4. "Skiing Earns Way to Sports Lead in State," *Oakland Tribune*, January 10, 1937.
5. Kehrlein, "Tahoe Region Ski Paradise."
6. Gregory, "California Skilands."
7. Lert, "Season in Review," 191.
8. Bradford, "Nevada," 11.
9. White, "Reporter's Tahoe Ski Marathon."
10. Lund, "Pure Gold," 120.

Chapter 1

11. Scott, *Saga of Lake Tahoe*, 19.
12. Ibid.
13. Magee, "Snowshoe Traveling in the Sierras"; Magee, "May in the Sierras."
14. Magee, "Snowshoe Traveling in the Sierras."

15. Muir, "Lake Tahoe in Winter," 119. Prior to 1930, skis were sometimes referred to as snowshoes and later on, to minimize confusion, referred to as Norwegian snowshoes. Snowshoes, as we know them today, were then referred to as Canadian snowshoes.
16. Ibid., 124.
17. Ibid., 125.
18. Pillsbury, "Through the High Sierra on Skies," 236.
19. Ibid., 239.
20. Ibid.
21. Ibid., 241.
22. Church, "Lake Tahoe in Winter," 274.
23. Ibid., 275.
24. Clark, "New Ski Sun Rises," 510.

Chapter 2

25. The club was not affiliated with the Sierra Club, though many of its members were.
26. Hildebrand, "History of Skiing in California," 72.
27. Bradley, "James S. Hutchinson," 14.
28. Pettit, "Homemade Sanctuary of Brotherly Love," 225.
29. Ibid.
30. *Olla Podrida, Sierra Ski Club*, scrapbook in the Sierra Club Colby Library, 9.
31. Hildebrand, "History of Skiing in California," 72.
32. *Sierra Club Reminiscences*, 8–9.
33. Harold C. Bradley letter, July 27, 1958, Sierra Club Mss., University of California, Berkeley, Bancroft Library.
34. Clair Tappaan Lodge Committee Meeting minutes, October 15, 1955, Sierra Club Mss., University of California, Berkeley, Bancroft Library.
35. Ibid.

Chapter 3

36. "Selling Snow," *California Magazine of the Pacific*, December 1936, 18.
37. Kelley, "Winter Sports in California," 4.
38. Ibid., 5.

39. "The Truckee Ice Carnival," *Reno Weekly Gazette and Stockman*, January 30, 1896.
40. Barkan, "Skiing in California," 39.
41. Ibid., 40.
42. Ibid., 42.
43. Clark, "New Ski Sun Rises," 510.
44. Brower, *Sierra Club Handbook*, 46.
45. Ibid., 40.
46. Ibid.
47. Ibid.
48. *Snow Sports Manual of the Sierra Club*, in *Olla Podrida Sierra Ski Club*, 118.
49. *Sierra Club Reminiscences*, 10.
50. Hildebrand, "Ski Heil," 2.
51. Schagen, "Center for Summer and Snow Activities," 9.
52. Johnny Ellis Archive, Donner Summit Historical Society, Norm Sayler Collection.
53. Johnny Ellis personal correspondence, Johnny Ellis Archive, Donner Summit Historical Society, Norm Sayler Collection.
54. Johnny Ellis Archive, Donner Summit Historical Society, Norm Sayler Collection.
55. Hildebrand, "Ski Heil," 1.
56. Brower, *Sierra Club Handbook*, 50.
57. Lert and Lund, "Bill Klein in Donner Pass."
58. Ibid., 21.
59. Ibid., 20.
60. Picard, "Peter Picard on the Early Donner Days," 2.
61. Clark, "Plans for Clair Tappaan Lodge," 3.
62. Clair Tappaan Lodge Committee Meeting minutes, September 19, 1953, Sierra Club Mss., University of California, Berkeley, Bancroft Library.
63. Degenhardt and Hughes, *Dinner with George*, 28.
64. McGillicuddy, "Warming Hut," 12.
65. Sierra Club Clair Tappaan Lodge Committee, Treasurers' Annual Report for Fiscal Year 1963–64, Sierra Club Mss., University of California, Berkeley, Bancroft Library.

Chapter 4

66. Burroughs Resort brochure, n.d.

67. "Business Meet of Ski Club Is Huge Success," *Sierra Sun and Truckee Republican*, November 24, 1938.
68. "Tahoe City," *Auburn Journal*, November 16, 1939.
69. "Tahoe Ski Club Is Making Progress on Winter Sports Hill," *Sierra Sun and Truckee Republican*, October 10, 1940.
70. "Much Work Done, Planned on Ski Hill at Tahoe," *Sierra Sun and Truckee Republican*, October 31, 1946.
71. Meadows, "Deer Park Ski Area."
72. "Deer Park Resort Builds a Poma Lift," *Tahoe Tattler*, November 1, 1957.
73. "Free Skiing December 21 at New Powder Bowl," *Tahoe Tattler*, December 20, 1957.
74. "Barrell Stave Olympics," *Skiing Magazine*, November 1963, 10W.
75. "Barrel Stave Slalom Set for Powder Bowl," *Placer Herald*, February 8, 1962.
76. Ottenheimer, "Small Ski Spas."
77. Meadows, "Deer Park Ski Area on Horns of a Dilemma."
78. Ibid.
79. Ibid.
80. Hubbard, "Skiing in the Tahoe Area."
81. Heath, "Wayne Poulsen," 23.
82. Ibid.
83. Cleese, "Native's Guide to the Nearby Slopes," 35.
84. "Papoose Is on the Loose," *Tahoe City World*, December 29, 1967.
85. Scott, "Man from Squaw," 21–22.
86. Wayne Poulsen Jr., email correspondence with the author, August 17, 2019.

Chapter 5

87. United States Department of Agriculture, "Highway 50 Corridor."
88. Turrentine Jackson and Pisani, *From Resort Area to Urban Recreation Center*, 6.
89. Hartwick, "Lake Tahoe Pioneer," 22.
90. Mitchell, *Strawberry*, xii.
91. Ibid., 103.
92. Falk, "Highway 50 to Be Open," 130.
93. Letter from Scollay Parker to Charles Pavka, March 19, 1965, National Archives at San Bruno, California.

94. Bowker, "Strawberry Lodge."
95. Letter from Herb Brook to Ethel Van Degrift, October 2, 1947, Ethel Van Degrift Collection, California Ski Library.
96. Ibid.
97. Watters, "Essay on Strawberry Ski Hut."
98. "The Edelweiss Plans Major Area at Lover's Leap Ridge," *The Skier*, February 1953, 6.
99. "You Are Invited to Participate in a Chair Lift for Edelweiss," n.p., n.d., 3, Donner Summit Historical Society, Norm Sayler Collection.
100. El Dorado National Forest Memo, February 28, 1963, National Archives, San Bruno, California.
101. Letter to Honorable Craig Hosmer, House of Representatives, from Chief Forester Edward P. Cliff, November 18, 1963, National Archives, San Bruno, California.
102. Letter to Forest Supervisor, Eldorado National Forest, from W.S. Davis, Assistant Regional Forester, October 21, 1964, National Archives, San Bruno, California.
103. Quoted in Yohalem, *"I Remember…"*, 164.
104. *Skier's Handbook 1947*, 224.
105. Kerhlein, "State Snowplows Clear Highway 50."
106. "New Lodge at Echo Lake," *Ski Heil*, March 1939, 24.
107. Ibid.
108. Macintosh, "Skiers, Two Snow Ploughs."
109. Sanford, "Echo Lake Chalet," 34.
110. Devencenzi, "Photographs and Memories."
111. Lindsay, "Haven Jorgensen Qualifies."
112. Hubbard, "Skiing in the Tahoe Area."
113. Sanford, "Echo Lake Chalet," 35.
114. Eisenberg, "Army Fate Puts Ex-Soldiers in Ski Business."
115. Nesbit, "Outdoors."
116. Ross, "War Enemies Are Peace Buddies."
117. Aynedter, "Juniors Moving Up Front," 6.
118. Ibid.
119. Ottenheimer, "Small Ski Spas."
120. Phipps, *Final Environmental Impact Statement*, 42.
121. USDA Forest Service, "Draft Environmental Impact Statement," 40.
122. Phipps, *Final Environmental Impact Statement*, S-1.
123. Ibid., S-2.
124. "Tahoe Group Names Officers," *Reno Gazette-Journal*, June 29, 1939.

125. Schneider and Foeger, *Ski Area Survey*, 5.
126. "Bijou Park Has Lake Frontage," *Placerville Mountain Democrat*, May 19, 1941.
127. Quoted in Frohlich, *Mountain Dreamers*, 68.
128. "Sierra Love Affair," *Skiing Magazine*, December 1960, 64.
129. "Lengthy Ski Lift Planned for Spooners District by Management of Glenbrook," *Nevada State Journal*, August 4, 1946.
130. Ibid.
131. Ibid.
132. Berry, "White Hills Ski."

Chapter 6

133. Federal Writers' Project, *WPA Guide to California*, 566.
134. "Donner Area Leads in Ski Lift Devices," *Auburn Journal*, February 3, 1941.
135. Peattie, *Sierra Nevada*, 238.
136. "Skiers Take to Slope Routes in Large Numbers," *California-Nevada Ski News and Sportsman*, December 21, 1948.
137. Donner Summit Winter Sports Committee, Press Release from Lykke-Wilkin & Associates, no date, Ethel Van Degrift Collection, Folder 17.1.
138. Santoro, "Auburn Ski Leap Novel."
139. DeWitt Nelson, interviewed by Amelia R. Fry. In University of California, Berkley Bancroft Library, Regional Oral History Office, *Management of Natural Resources in California* 1925–1966, 1976, 72.
140. "Funicula Americana," *Ski Bulletin*, March 29, 1935, 6.
141. "Novel Ski Equipment," *Placer Herald*, February 5, 1938.
142. Kehrlein, "Skiers Need Labor Saving Devices."
143. "Cisco Tunnel Mountain Area Made Ready for 1955–56 Skiing Season," *Placer Herald*, November 17, 1955.
144. "Auburn Ski Club Grounds Leased by Corporation," *Auburn Journal*, November 17, 1955.
145. "Auction Slated for Ski Lodges, Equipment," *Press-Tribune*, August 11, 1960.
146. Advertisement, *San Francisco Examiner*, January 21, 1960.
147. "Two Million Expected to Enjoy Annual Winter Sports," *San Francisco Examiner*, December 12, 1937.
148. Johnny Ellis, correspondence to his family, October 1937, Johnny Ellis Archive, Donner Summit Historical Society, Norm Sayler Collection.

149. Bob Blake, "Snow, Ice Conditions in State," *Oakland Tribune*, January 29, 1939.
150. Ibid.
151. "Summit Lakes Property Sold," *Reno Gazette-Journal*, June 29, 1945.
152. Strickland, "Norden."
153. Norm Sayler, interview with the author, Norden, California, October 3, 2019.
154. "T-bar Now Operating," *Serene Lakes News*, February 1967.
155. Lund, "The 1930s."
156. According to Annette Hofmann, German sport historian, "The term Skiwart is hard to translate. It is sort of old fashioned, but I would say it is something like a person that is responsible in a ski club for the skiing section, sometimes even a ski instructor, but it doesn't have to be."
157. "Winter Sports May Be Dropped by Local Group," *Sierra Sun and Truckee Republican*, October 6, 1938.
158. "Fate of Local Winter Sports to be Settled," *Sierra Sun and Truckee Republican*, November 17, 1938.
159. "Winter Sports to Be Continued by Two Local Youths," *Sierra Sun and Truckee Republican*, November 24, 1938.
160. "Plans Progress on Local Winter Sports Program," *Sierra Sun and Truckee Republican*, May 30, 1940.
161. "Financial Aid Promised for Winter Sports," *Sierra Sun and Truckee Republican*, August 8, 1940.
162. "Goal Near in Drive for Snow Sport Fund," *Press-Tribune*, September 18, 1940.
163. "Ski Hill Near Completion as Plans Progress," *Sierra Sun and Truckee Republican*, November 21, 1940.
164. "District Plans to Sell Local Winter Sports Property," *Sierra Sun and Truckee Republican*, August 24, 1944.
165. *Skier's Handbook 1947*, 223.
166. Richnak, "Life after Death."
167. Bunker, "Planners Roll Out Hilltop Proposal."
168. Truckee Homes for Active | Sierra Sotheby's International Realty, www.sierrasothebyrealty.com/eng/sales/truckee-ca-usa.

BIBLIOGRAPHY

Aynedter, Lutz. "Juniors Moving Up Front." *The Skier*, April 1, 1952.

Barkan, Otto. "Skiing in California." *Sierra Club Bulletin*, February 1931.

Beesley, David. "Reconstructing the Landscape: An Environmental History, 1820–1960." Aspen Bibliography, Paper 1804, 1996.

Berry, Bill. "White Hills Ski." *Nevada State Journal*, December 8, 1946.

Berry, William B., and Chapman Wentworth. *Lost Sierra: Gold, Ghosts & Skis*. Soda Springs, CA: Western Skisport Museum, 1991.

Bowker, Michael. "Strawberry Lodge: A Sports Center for All Seasons." *San Francisco Examiner*, April 6, 1986.

Bradford, Wayne. "Nevada." *The Skier*, January 1950.

Bradley, Harold. "James S. Hutchinson, Sierra Pioneer." *Sierra Club Bulletin*, November 1959.

Brower, David, ed. *The Sierra Club Handbook*. San Francisco: Sierra Club, 1947,

Bunker, David. "Planners Roll Out Hilltop Proposal." *Sierra Sun*, January 29, 2004.

Caldwell, Peter. *Echo Lake Reflections: A Photographic and Historical Journey*. Honolulu, HI: Taote Publishing, 2004.

Church, James E. "Lake Tahoe in Winter." *Sierra Club Bulletin*, January 1915.

Clark, Lewis F. "A New Ski Sun Rises." *Appalachia*, bulletin of the Appalachian Mountain Club, December 1933.

———. "Plans for Clair Tappaan Lodge." *Sierra Club Bulletin*, December 1941.

Cleese, Rose Marie. "A Native's Guide to the Nearby Slopes." *San Francisco Magazine*, December 1973.

Colby, William E., "Clair Sprague Tappaan." *Sierra Club Bulletin*, February 1933.

Degenhardt, Helen, and Noreen Hughes. *Dinner with George*. n.p., n.d. California Ski Library, Norco, CA.

Devencenzi, Liz. "Photographs and Memories: A Conversation with Long-Time Tahoe Resident, Haven Jorgensen." Photocopy, no publication information. California Ski Library, Norco, CA.

Eisenberg, Marvin. "Army Fate Puts Ex-Soldiers in Ski Business." *San Francisco Call Bulletin*, January 20, 1950.

Elkins, Frank, and Frank Harper, eds. *World Ski Book*. New York: Longmans, Green & Company, 1949.

Falk, Jane. "Highway 50 to Be Open for All-Year Travel." In *Western Ski Annual 1941–42*, ed. William McKinley Stensaas. Modesto, CA: Western Ski Annual Publishing Company, 1941.

Federal Writers' Project of the Works Progress Administration for the State of California. *The WPA Guide to California*. New York: Pantheon Books, 1984.

Frohlich, Robert. *Mountain Dreamers: Visionaries of Sierra Nevada Skiing*. Truckee, CA: Coldstream Press, 1997.

Gillis, John R. "Tunnels of the Pacific Railroad." *Transactions of the American Society of Civil Engineers* 1 (1872): 156–57.

Gregory, G.H. "California Skilands." *New York Times*, December 5, 1948.

Greuner, Lorene. *Lake Valley's Past: A Guide to Twenty Historical Sites at Tahoe's South Shore*. South Lake Tahoe, CA: Lake Tahoe Historical Society, 1971.

Hartwick, Kathy. "Lake Tahoe Pioneer." *Far West Ski News*, October 15, 1976.

Heath, Ed. "Wayne Poulsen—Skimaster of Reno." *Ski Heil*, February 1940.

Hildebrand, Joel H. "A History of Ski-ing in California." In *British Ski Year Book 1939*, ed. Arnold Lunn. London: Ski Club of Great Britain, 1939.

———. "Ski Heil." *Sierra Club Bulletin*, February 1935.

Hill, Cortlandt T. *Skier's Handbook*. Los Angeles: Ramsden's Press, 1947.

Hubbard, Jim. "Skiing in the Tahoe Area–The Early Days." Stardust Lake Tahoe, www.stardust-tahoe.com.

Hutchinson, Lincoln. "Skiing in the High Sierras: California Ski Club Accepts the Challenge of the Snow." *American Forests and Forest Life* 36, no. 1 (January 1930).

Kehrlein, Oliver. "Skiers Need Labor Saving Devices." *San Francisco Examiner*, March 5, 1938.

———. "State Snowplows Clear Highway 50." *San Francisco Examiner*, March 7, 1941.

———. "Tahoe Region Ski Paradise." *San Francisco Examiner*, December 13, 1938

Kelley, Dr. Norman D. "Winter Sports in California as Taken by the Sierra Club." *California Out-of-Doors*, December 1914.

Lert, Wolfgang. "The Season in Review." In *American Ski Annual 1949*. Brattleboro, VT: Stephen Daye Press, 1949.

Lert, Wolfgang, and Morten Lund. "Bill Klein in Donner Pass: A Ski Teacher from Beginning to End." *Skiing Heritage*, June 1999.

Lindsay, Shauna. "Haven Jorgensen Qualifies as a Ski Pioneer at Tahoe." Photocopy, no publication information. California Ski Library, Norco, CA.

Lund, Morten. "Pure Gold." *SKI Magazine*, December 1973.

———. "The 1930s: The Unexpected Blossoming of Alpine Skiing," International Skiing History Organization, skiinghistory.org.

Macintosh, Charlie. "Skiers, Two Snow Ploughs Open Echo Summit Highway." *Oakland Tribune*, March 19, 1941.

Magee, Thomas. "May in the Sierras." *San Francisco Call*, May 5, 1895.

———. "Snowshoe Traveling in the Sierras." *San Francisco Call*, April 5, 1896.

McGillicuddy, Bob. "Warming Hut: Solid Comfort on Signal Hill." *Sierra Club Bulletin*, February 1956.

Meadows, Bruce. "Deer Park Ski Area on Horns of a Dilemma." *Press Democrat*, December 7, 1984.

Mitchell, Richard L. *Strawberry: Valley of Legends*. Sonoma, CA: Pezzo Unico Publishing, 2017.

Mohler, Chaco. *Heavenly Dreams: The Making of a Mountain*. n.p., n.d. California Ski Library, Norco, CA.

Muir, John. "Lake Tahoe in Winter." *Sierra Club Bulletin*, May 1900.

Nesbit, Mark. "Outdoors." *Palo Alto Times*, February 16, 1950.

North, Arthur W. "California's Norseland: Where One May Enjoy the Winter Sports of the Adirondacks." *Sunset Magazine*, March 1906.

Olla Podrida, Sierra Ski Club. Oakland, CA: William E. Colby Library, 1925.

Ottenheimer, Miles. "Small Ski Spas Feeling Deep Financial Pinch." *San Francisco Examiner*, April 10, 1966

Peattie, Roderick, ed. *The Sierra Nevada: The Range of Light*. New York: Vanguard Press, 1947.

Pettit, G.A. "The Homemade Sanctuary of Brotherly Love." *California Monthly*, December 1926.

Phipps, John. *Final Environmental Impact Statement and Record of Decision on Future Use of the Echo Summit Ski Area Site*. United States Department of Agriculture, Forest Service, March 1993.

Picard, Peter. "Peter Picard on Early Donner Days." *Skiing Heritage*, September 1999.

Pillsbury, Arthur C. "Through the High Sierra on Skies." *Camera Craft*, April 1902.

Richnak, Barbara. "Life after Death for Nation's Oldest Winter Ski Resort." *Tahoe World*, March 2, 1978.

Ross, George. "War Enemies Are Peace Buddies." *Oakland Tribune*, January 23, 1955.

Sanford, Jill. "Echo Lake Chalet." *Sierra Heritage*, October 2015.

Santoro, Al. "Auburn Ski Leap Novel, Thrilling Sport." *Oakland Post-Enquirer*, February 20, 1934.

Schagen, John P. "Center for Summer and Snow Activities." *Sierra Club Bulletin*, May 1956.

Schneider, Hannes, and Luggi Foeger. *Ski Area Survey of California and Parts of Nevada and Oregon*. 1946.

Scott, E.B. *The Saga of Lake Tahoe*. Lake Tahoe, CA: Sierra-Tahoe Publishing Company, 1957.

———. *The Saga of Lake Tahoe*. Vol. 2. Lake Tahoe, CA: Sierra-Tahoe Publishing Company, 1973.

Scott, Jim. "Man from Squaw." *Skiing Magazine*, January 1962.

Shea, Liz. "Winter at Norden." *Sierra Club Bulletin*, November 1956.

Sierra Club Reminiscences: Joel Hildebrand: Sierra Club Leader and Ski Mountaineer. Berkeley, CA: Sierra Club History Committee, University of California, 1974.

Skier's Handbook 1947. Los Angeles: Ramsden's Press, 1947.

Strickland, Bill. "Norden." *Sierra Sun and Truckee Republican*, December 12, 1959.

"Tappaan Lodge Continues to Grow." *Sierra Club Bulletin*, October 1939.

Turrentine Jackson, W., and Donald J. Pisani. *From Resort Area to Urban Recreation Center: Themes in the Development of Lake Tahoe 1946–1956*. Davis, CA: Institute of Governmental Affairs, April 1973.

United States Department of Agriculture. "Draft Environmental Impact Statement on the Future Use of Echo Summit Ski Area Site." September 1992.

———. "The Highway 50 Corridor: America's Gateway to the West." El Dorado National Forest, www.fs.usda.gov/eldorado.

Vestal, Lee. *The Celio Family in Lake Valley*. South Lake Tahoe, CA: Lake Tahoe Historical Society, 2015.

Watters, Charles "Muddy." "An Essay on Strawberry Ski Hut." *Donner Trail–Sierra Nevada Sportsman*, April 27, 1948.

White, Kit Carson. "Reporter's Tahoe Ski Marathon." *San Francisco Examiner*, December 20, 1964.

Yohalem, Betty. *"I Remember"...Stories and Pictures of El Dorado County Pioneer Families*. Placerville, CA: El Dorado County Chamber of Commerce, 1977.

INDEX

C

D

E

F

G

H

J

K

L

M

N

O

P

R

S

T

U

V

W

Y

Z

ABOUT THE AUTHOR

Ingrid P. Wicken is the leading authority on the history of skiing in Southern California and has written four books: *Pray for Snow: The History of Skiing in Southern California* (2002), *Skiing in Southern California* (2007), *Lost Ski Areas of Southern California* (2012) and *50 Years of Flight: Ski Jumping in California 1900–1950* (2017). In 2004, she founded the California Ski Library (www.skilibrary.com), one of the finest collections of books, historic photographs, magazines, annuals, brochures, catalogues, programs, newsletters and other ephemera in the United States. She has won multiple awards for her work preserving and documenting skiing history. She was awarded the Far West Ski Association's Western Ski Heritage Award in 2002, 2005, 2013 and 2018 and the Western Snowsports Builder Award in 2018 for the founding of the Ski Library. The International Ski History Association has also recognized her published work, awarding her the Skade Award in 2003, 2008, 2015 and 2018. She is a professor emerita of kinesiology at Moreno Valley College.